1990

MEN WITH GUNS &

love
Adam.

of related interest

SAYLES ON SAYLES
edited by Gavin Smith

Men with Guns & Lone Star

JOHN SAYLES

faber and faber

First published in 1998
by Faber and Faber Limited
3 Queen Square London WC1N 3AU

Photoset by Parker Typesetting Service, Leicester
Printed in England by Clays Ltd, St Ives plc

© John Sayles, 1998

Photographs of *Men with Guns* and *Lone Star* © Alan Pappe, 1998

John Sayles is hereby identified as author of this
work in accordance with Section 77 of the Copyright,
Designs and Patents Act 1988

A CIP record for this book
is available from the British Library
ISBN 0–571–19527–X

2 4 6 8 10 9 7 5 3 1

Contents

INTRODUCTION

The screenplays for *Lone Star* and *Men with Guns* represent the blueprints for movies about a lone man on a quest. As the main protagonist in each searches for their very personal resolution, they serve as guides for us, leading us into wider social and political arenas. The tone and pace of the two films are very distinct, and though in one the dialogue is mostly in English and in the other mostly in Spanish, their main differences lie elsewhere.

The backbone of *Lone Star* is the definition of personal identity through family history for a white county sheriff, an African-American army colonel and a Chicana high school teacher. The trigger for this is the discovery of the remains of a former sheriff, evidently murdered. The structure of the detective story serves as the vehicle to carry us through the past and present social structure of a Texas border town, with surprises in store for each of the three. It is Sam Deeds, the white sheriff, who digs the story out for us. He is a man ignorant of history – personal and social – through no fault of his own. Lies have been told, secrets kept, history passed on in a deliberately distorted fashion. Once Sam begins to untangle truth from legend he is faced with a second challenge – the responsibility of supporting or attacking the 'official story'.

Men with Guns is also driven by a search. Dr Fuentes, a wealthy, relatively liberal society physician, has trained several young students to become 'barefoot' doctors and work with the poorest of his nation's people in the countryside. When he discovers a former student selling drugs in a slum and hears that all might not be going well with the health program, he sets out to find his other students in their remote villages. Fuentes is also ignorant of history – but this time it's a careless, even willful ignorance, that of the man who subconsciously does not want to know. Confronted with new evidence of genocide in each village he visits, Fuentes is drawn further and further into the dark heart of his own society's violence, until there is no honorable way he can return to his former life.

Sam Deeds also ends up at a point of no return, knowledge

forcing him into decisions that will seal him off from the society that raised him. But he does get to make that decision, and the universe he inhabits is a less fatalistic one than the world of *Men with Guns*.

My image for Sam's action in *Lone Star* was circular, a kind of digging through layers, always moving toward a center of truth. The image for Dr Fuentes' quest is linear, a straight journey leading him further away from the comforts and distractions of his city and social life, and deeper into a black and white world of powerful versus powerless. *Lone Star* is very much about the specifics of a very particular place and history – the Texas/Mexican border with its baggage of wars and racial politics. *Men with Guns*, from its bluntly simplistic title to the generic quality of the place names Fuentes visits, is meant to be more universal, more starkly basic in its reality. Though legend is invoked in *Lone Star*, the story itself is steeped in detail and idiosyncracy. The characters in *Men with Guns* have the feel of real human beings caught in a horrific fable.

In writing *Men with Guns* my mental geography for Fuentes' trip was in terms of products and crops. We leave a huge glass and plastic city to cross an arid plain where desperate people sell salt by the roadside. We cut through flat, humid sugarcane country. We cross rivers, then start to climb foothills covered with coffee and bananas. Finally we leave the road behind and climb by foot up into the steep mountain rainforest, slashed and burned for meager cornfields, until we reach the jungle canopy at the summit. Fuentes makes a kind of Pilgrim's Progress, a journey where each turn brings new hardship and new knowledge. It is no odyssey, however, no way for him to bring back the news to his old home and live on as a wiser man. His questions at first belie his ignorance – ignorance of the people he meant to help; ignorance of the nature and extremity of his own government; ignorance even of the limited penetration of his own language. The answers he receives, when people are willing to talk, are mostly direct and a bit condescending. How could you not know the answer to this? Only Padre Portillo, the only other educated man he meets along the way, is enigmatic and metaphoric with him at first.

Sam Deeds constantly asks questions as well, specific evidence-seeking questions, but almost never receives a direct answer.

Where the answer in *Men with Guns* is almost always simpler and more brutal than Fuentes had thought, the answer in *Lone Star* is almost always more complex and paradoxical than Sam has wanted to believe. The witnesses Sam grills aren't only necessary to hide information with their metaphors, they're trying to get him to see the world in all its contradictions and conflicts of interest.

My interest in the border probably started when as a kid I saw Fess Parker play Davy Crockett on TV. The legend of the Alamo, a handful of freedom-loving patriots holding out unto death against a whole army of foreign invaders, was particularly strong to me, and has been a central theme in the way white Texans see and portray themselves. As I got older, delved further into the actual history of the region and spent time on the border, a different, more complex and, to me, more interesting picture emerged. The contradiction of men fighting for the freedom to, among other things, own slaves, seemed so far from the official version that I felt here were some bones that needed digging up. The people I met on the border, with their complicated alliances and classes of self-identification (the Mexican-American and his Mexican cousin five hundred yards across the river have come to think of themselves in very different ways), led me to my characters of Sam, Del and Pilar, who all get more than they bargained for when they examine their own roots.

Men with Guns started with stories told to me by friends – one whose uncle was a doctor, the other whose father was an agronomist – both who trained people for programs in Latin America for the best of intentions with the worst of results. That basic idea – how does a person deal with the responsibility of putting somebody else at mortal risk? – formed the personal core of the story. The theme I found in the troubled world around us – over sixty percent of Americans stated they wanted no messy details from the press during the Gulf War; the various civil wars and genocides in Central and South America, in the Balkans, in Africa, in the former Soviet Union; the untenable position of civilian villagers caught between US troops and Viet Cong in the Vietnam conflict. Whereas the quest in *Lone Star* reveals layers of complexity and interdependence, life in *Men with Guns* boils down to a dynamic as old as human society – men who have weapons and are willing to use them have power over those who don't. The story is full of groups who define themselves and are defined in very distinct categories – white versus indigenous, indigenous versus Ladino (Indian people who speak Spanish and dress in Western clothes), rich versus poor, army versus guerrilla, each language group against the other – but, as a potentially loaded pistol changes hands again and again, the most basic and important difference is who is packing and who isn't.

The version of *Men with Guns* that follows is also a translation from Spanish and various indigenous languages into subtitle format. This structure of no more than thirty-six characters and spaces per line and no more than two lines per screen lends a haiku-like simplicity to most of the dialogue, in contrast with the more vernacular liveliness of the American tourists' speech. The spoken dialogue, though still relatively direct and unadorned, is much looser and more colorful in its own idiom than what the reader will find here.

I tend not to editorialize too much in screenplays; I don't use a whole lot of physical or thematic description. Reading these without having reference to the movies made from them may be a little stark. The music is not here, the acting, the visceral power of the locations, no camera movement or lighting – all the things that make a movie a movie. So try to take them as the blueprints they are, outlines that helped people come together and make a story.

John Sayles, 1997

MEN WITH GUNS

CREDITS

DR FUENTES	Federico Luppi
DOMINGO	Damián Delgado
RABBIT	Dan Rivera González
GRACIELA	Tania Cruz
PADRE PORTILLO	Damián Alcázar
HARRIET	Kathryn Grody
ANDREW	Mandy Patinkin

Written, directed and edited by	John Sayles
Produced by	R. Paul Miller
	Maggie Renzi
Executive Producers	Lou Gonda
	Jody Patton
	John Sloss
Director of Photography	Slawomir Idziak
Production Designer	Felipe Fernández del Paso
Costume Design	Mayes C. Rubeo
Original Music	Mason Daring
Casting	Lizzie Curry Martinez

EXT. CLEARING – PRE-DAWN

CU: fire.

We see the hands of a Young Girl and of her Mother as they pile kindling and start a cookfire. The sun won't rise for another couple hours.

> MOTHER
> This will burn fast – use it only to start the flame. Then this will last the morning.

> YOUNG GIRL
> Tell me more about the man.

The Mother waits till the kindling has taken flame before she speaks.

> MOTHER
> He has trouble breathing – sometimes he fights to swallow air. He can put his hand on you and tell what your sickness is.

YOUNG GIRL

By magic?

MOTHER

By science. He's a doctor who lives in the city.

YOUNG GIRL

Can he cure you of worms?

MOTHER

City people don't get sick like we do. They speak a different language, they wear different clothes –

INT. DOCTOR'S OFFICE – DAY

CU: 'Invisible Man'.

We see a large chart of the human body, stripped of its skin, muscles and veins visible in bright colors.

MOTHER

– they don't look anything like us.

We rack focus to see a man of seventy bent over an examination table – the General.

GENERAL

The people – the common people – love drama.

CU: finger.

We see a hand in a rubber glove, one finger buried in a jar of a Vaseline.

FUENTES
(*off-screen*)

True. They watch soap operas.

Two-shot: Dr Fuentes puts the greased finger up the General's rectum, checking for something.

GENERAL

Which is why you can't believe any of these rumors. How is it?

> FUENTES

It doesn't seem to have changed.

> GENERAL

It isn't bigger?

> FUENTES

It isn't smaller, either. We'll have to watch it.

> GENERAL

What a thought – watching my ass.

The two laugh.

The Reds make up these stories and the people believe them. It makes our job even harder.

> FUENTES

You can get dressed.

> GENERAL

Thanks.

The General puts his clothes in order.

I was sorry to hear about your wife.

> FUENTES

Thank you. There was nothing we could do.

> GENERAL

You're retiring soon?

> FUENTES

I don't know. My vacation starts tomorrow. I'll have time to think.

> GENERAL

Going to the beach?

> FUENTES

Somewhere new. Without Isabel – maybe the mountains.

The General puts his uniform jacket on and we can see the stars on his shoulder and collar. A powerful man.

GENERAL

The mountains? My Tigers spend half their lives chasing guerrillas in those fucking mountains.

FUENTES

I thought you'd wiped them out, that the guerrillas were only a rumor –

GENERAL

It only takes a couple of those bastards to make trouble. What can you do in the mountains?

Fuentes smiles slightly.

So tell me – my condition –

FUENTES

– is confidential. As always.

GENERAL

It could be used against me.

FUENTES

Who'd want to give you trouble?

The General puts his hand on the doctor's shoulder.

GENERAL

You're like a child, Humberto. The world is a savage place.

EXT. CAFÉ – DAY

We start on the impassive face of an Indian Busboy, waiting to swoop onto whatever table needs his attention.

ANGELA
(*off-screen*)

But you love the beach.

FUENTES
(*off-screen*)

Nothing lasts at the beach. The waves wipe it all away.

ANGELA
(*off-screen*)

That's why people like it. They can forget their problems.
And you alone, without Mami –

We shift to see Fuentes, sitting with his daughter Angela and her fiancé
Raul, at a café in a courtyard in the center of the city.

FUENTES

I've been thinking about my students in the Program.

ANGELA

Daddy trained doctors for the Government –

FUENTES

Ambassadors of Health.

RAUL

I remember something about that – foreigners who made war
on tapeworms –

FUENTES
(*proud*)

The Alliance for Progress.

RAUL

I don't know why they don't go cure their own Indians.

ANGELA

Raul –

RAUL

The Government was forced to accept their aid to shut the
Americans up.

FUENTES

That might be true, but the Program was a good idea.

ANGELA

You should be really proud, Daddy.

FUENTES

I'd like to visit some of my students.

ANGELA

In the countryside?

RAUL

If they're still there.

FUENTES

Why wouldn't they be?

RAUL

It's been, what, two years?

FUENTES

Three.

RAUL

Three years with Indians. My idea of hell.

FUENTES

It isn't a punishment –

RAUL

Doctor, how many of your patients are Indians?

Fuentes thinks. He can't name one.

My family has been living with them at our ranch for centuries. The more you do for them or give them, the lazier they get. Giving them a taste of modern things – ideas, medicine, television – you just destroy their souls.

FUENTES

The Program was a good idea! A good idea! It's my legacy.

RAUL

Have your students written to you?

A moment of silence.

FUENTES

No, they haven't, but –

ANGELA

Maybe the beach – but in a smaller hotel.

INT. WAITING ROOM – DAY

Two Rich Women sit waiting for the doctor.

> RICH WOMAN I
>
> My kidneys are bothering me, too. When I drink red wine I
> get a pain right here –
> > (*indicates*)
> The more expensive the wine the sharper the pain.

> RICH WOMAN 2
>
> How awful!

Fuentes passes through the room.

> RICH WOMEN
> > (*together*)
> Good afternoon, Doctor!

> FUENTES
>
> Good afternoon.

Fuentes exits.

> RICH WOMAN 2
> The doctor doesn't look so good.

EXT. CITY – LATE AFTERNOON

*Fuentes walks toward us, seen with a long lens. At almost every corner
there is a poor Indian, begging for change with open palm. Fuentes, lost
in his thoughts, puts a few coins in the hand of one beggar without
looking at her.*

FLASHBACK: INT. MEDICAL CLASSROOM – DAY

*We hear Fuentes lecturing as we rack across the faces of young medical
students – Cienfuegos, Montoya, Brazos, Arenas, Echevarria, De Soto,
Hidalgo – listening eagerly from their seats –*

> FUENTES
> > (*off-screen*)
> In a struggle against death, a small advantage in technology
> can win the battle. Cortes won an empire with a few men –

9

but he had the horse and the gun and his adversary didn't. Where you're going your principal enemies will be bacteria and ignorance. Bacterias can be fought with drugs, but their ally, ignorance –

We pan to see Fuentes, standing in front of a blackboard bearing complicated Latin words and chemical descriptions of antibiotics.

Nobody is immune to this disease. More specifically, we expect you not only to apply your medical knowledge but also –

Fuentes's voice fades, replaced by the sounds of a TV game show.

INT. FUENTES'S HOUSE – NIGHT

Fuentes stands, lost in thought, in his living room, the TV playing a stupid game show. He snaps out of his reverie, looks around. We follow him into his study, carrying a drink in his hand.

INT. STUDY – NIGHT

CU: photograph of Fuentes with the students, smiling for the camera. Fuentes pulls it off the wall.

Wider: Fuentes looks at the picture, remembering.

FUENTES
It was an excellent idea.

FADE OUT

EXT. MARKET – DAY

Fuentes looks over the produce in a crowded open market. Many of the vendors are Indians, sitting behind their produce. Fuentes sees someone.

POV: Bravo. Bravo, twenty-five, is speaking with a Ladino vendor.

Before Fuentes can call out, Bravo starts away from the market, walking rapidly. Fuentes follows.

EXT. STREET – DAY

Fuentes tries to catch up to the younger man.

FUENTES

Bravo! Hey! Bravo!

We pan to see Bravo. He shoots an annoyed look back at the doctor, then hops onto a bus.

Wait!

INT. CAR — DAY

Fuentes drives, following the bus.

EXT. BARRIO — DUMP

We see a poor neighborhood behind a mountain of garbage.

EXT. STREET — DAY

Fuentes's car rolls toward us. He parks it in front of a shack made from scraps of corrugated metal.

INT. SHACK — DAY

Bravo piles boxes of appliances. Fuentes appears at the open doorway.

FUENTES

Bravo?

Bravo doesn't answer.

Don't you recognize me?

Bravo looks at the doctor with a mixture of resentment and shame.

BRAVO

What do you want with me?

FUENTES

Why aren't you in the village?

BRAVO

The Program is finished.

FUENTES

That's not true.

BRAVO

It's finished for me.

FUENTES

You were trained – you accepted the responsibility. Dozens of students who applied weren't as lucky as you.

BRAVO

I was lucky, all right. Luckier than Cienfuegos.

FUENTES

What happened to Cienfuegos?

BRAVO

What do you think?

FUENTES

I have no idea.

Bravo looks at him for a long moment, deciding whether to believe him.

BRAVO

He didn't get a warning.

FUENTES

A warning of what?

BRAVO
(*smiling bitterly*)

You don't know a thing about it, do you?

Fuentes looks around the squalid shack.

FUENTES

What are you doing living in Los Perdidos?

BRAVO

This is a pharmacy. We sell drugs at popular prices.

Fuentes gives him a look.

So your classes weren't a complete waste.

FUENTES
(*shaken*)

I sent you with medicine, training, with the support of the Government.

BRAVO

Dr Fuentes, you're the most learned man I've ever met. And the most ignorant.

Fuentes doesn't know what he's getting at.

Go find Cienfuegos. He's got the whole story.

Two Street Kids appear at the door, looking at Fuentes suspiciously.

Go home, Doctor. Los Perdidos is no place to be when the sun goes down.

INT. OFFICE – NIGHT

CU: chest.

Fuentes puts a stethoscope against his own bare chest.

Wider: Fuentes listens to his heart. He doesn't like what he hears.

He opens the door of a cabinet to see his supply of medicines. He pulls down various boxes and bottles, putting them into his black bag.

FADE OUT

FADE UP ON:

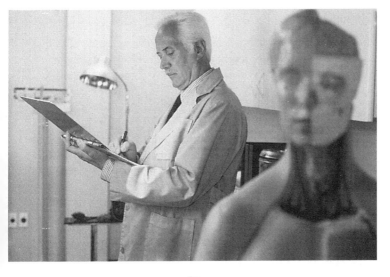

EXT. STREET – MORNING

Outside Fuentes's house in a wealthy neighborhood of the city. Fuentes loads the station wagon of his son Carlos.

CARLOS
Angela called me. Did you change your plans?

FUENTES
It was a shock. Bravo was one of my best students.

CARLOS
He got some Indian girl pregnant and had to run to save his ass.

Fuentes lifts his black bag.

Can I use the Mercedes till you're back?

EXT. ROAD – DAY

Fuentes drives on a dry plain, leaving the city. A truck bearing a rattling load of soda bottles (Kokal) passes him, honking. We see Mario and Jesus, the drivers, smiling and waving as they pass.

EXT. ROAD – DAY

CU: salt.

An Old Indian Man sells salt in plastic bags from a small table by the side of the road. There is nothing but dry plain for miles around. Fuentes speaks from the car window.

FUENTES
Hello. What town are you from?

OLD INDIAN MAN
From here.

FUENTES
But this place must have a name. What's it called?

The Old Man shrugs.

OLD INDIAN MAN
We're Salt People. This is where we live.

FUENTES
(*looking around*)
But there's nothing here.

OLD INDIAN MAN
You can't see anything from a car.

EXT. CAFÉ – DAY

A gas station and diner alongside the highway, cars parked in front.

INT. CAFÉ – DAY

CU: map.

We hear the voices of a pair of Americans, Andrew and Harriet, while a finger moves across a map of the country.

ANDREW
(*off-screen; English*)
There was like a hub here – like Chicago or Atlanta –

HARRIET
(*off-screen; English*)
They cut paths through the jungle?

Fuentes studies his menu as the tourists look at their map at the next table –

ANDREW
(*English*)
No jungle to cut through. It was all farmland back then. Overpopulated, overfarmed. Harriet, see if this guy knows –

HARRIET
(*Spanish*)
Excuse me, sir, do you know how far it is to the ruins in Jobal?

FUENTES
(*Spanish*)
I'm not sure. I've never travelled here before.

HARRIET
(*English*)
I think he said he doesn't know this area.

ANDREW
(*English*)
Great.

HARRIET
(*English*)
At least he speaks Spanish.
(*to Fuentes; Spanish*)
When we speak to the Indians they don't understand Spanish.

FUENTES
(*Spanish*)
I don't think the Indians in the United States speak English.

HARRIET
(*English*)
He wants to know if our Indians speak English.
(*to Fuentes; Spanish*)
I think all of them do.

(*to Andrew; English*)
I think there's a law, isn't there?

ANDREW
(*English*)
Ask if he's heard about any atrocities.

HARRIET
(*English*)
I can't ask him that.

ANDREW
(*English*)
Look, if we're going up there –

HARRIET
(*English*)
You ask him.

ANDREW
(*don't translate*)
Hay – it's hay, isn't it? Hay atrocidados aqui?

No response from Fuentes, confused.

Atrocidados?

HARRIET
(*Spanish*)
My husband wants to know if you've read about problems in this area. Political problems.

ANDREW
(*English*)
Tell him about the book we have, with the people with their hands cut off.
(*don't translate*)
Manos cutados –

HARRIET
(*don't translate*)
Cortados.

FUENTES
(*defensive; Spanish*)
That must be in another country. Not here.

ANDREW
(*Spanish*)
Not here?

FUENTES
(*Spanish*)
It isn't perfect here, but you can't believe all the stories.

HARRIET
(*Spanish*)
There are stories about the murders in the papers in New York.

FUENTES
(*smiling; Spanish*)
Newspapers are businesses. And the common people love drama.

HARRIET
(*Spanish*)
That's true.
(*English*)
He says the common people love drama.

ANDREW
(*English*)
Ask him why they don't have fajitas here.
(*don't translate*)
Que no – what's the word for fajitas?

EXT. ROAD – DAY

Fuentes drives through the beginning of a low, cane-growing area. We see workers slashing and burning cane, trucks full of stalks passing by.

EXT. ROAD – DAY

Fuentes has stopped at a fork in the road, hiding his bag, camera and suitcase under a blanket. An Indian Man walks by on the other side of the road. Fuentes calls to him.

FUENTES
Señor, is the town of Rio Seco close to here?

The Indian points left. There is no road, just a path through a cane field.

How do you get there?

The Indian points again to the same spot.

EXT. CANE FIELD – DAY

Fuentes walks through the cane, pausing a moment to rest.

EXT. VILLAGE – DAY

A dozen small houses. Chickens peck at the ground. All the inhabitants are Indian.

CU: Woman.

Women, hanging wet laundry in front of a house, look at Fuentes without expression.

FUENTES
Señora, excuse me. Do you know where Dr Cienfuegos lives? The doctor here – Cienfuegos – This is Rio Seco, isn't it? Señora!

The Women grab Children and shut themselves inside.

Various shots of Indian people.

Fuentes follows a Young Man between shacks.

FUENTES
Hey, listen to me, please –

The Young Man escapes. Fuentes turns and sees a Woman.

Señora, excuse me –

Fuentes calls to two Men crossing past the village.

Señores, do you know Dr Cienfuegos? Hey!

Fuentes approaches two Children on swings.

Hey there, this is Rio Seco, right?

The Children run.

Fuentes stands in a doorway.

Could you tell me where Dr Cienfuegos lives?

The door is slammed in his face.

Fuentes sits in front of an abandoned house, sweat rolling from his forehead.

It's like nobody speaks Spanish.

ABUELA
(*off-screen*)
Who's that? Who's out there?

Fuentes turns to see an old and blind woman, Abuela, sitting on the floor of the ruined house.

FUENTES
Señora, is this Rio Seco?

ABUELA
Of course it is. Are you blind?

She laughs.

FUENTES
I've never been here before. Nobody will talk to me.

ABUELA
We're just poor Sugar People here. Almost nobody visits.
Who are you?

FUENTES
I'm Dr Fuentes.

ABUELA
Good. We need a doctor, 'cause the last one died.

Fuentes is distressed to hear this.

FUENTES

Died? How?

ABUELA

They killed him.

FUENTES

Who killed him?

ABUELA

Them. Men with guns.

FUENTES

You saw this?

ABUELA
(*laughing*)

I'm blind.

FUENTES

I'm sorry.

ABUELA

But I know everything that happens. They made us witness –
even me. The doctor and three others – out there –

FUENTES

Somebody shot them?

ABUELA

They burned them with gasoline. I smelled it. First the gas,
then the fire and then the men. Cooked them all.

FUENTES

Why?

ABUELA

Because they had guns and we didn't.

FUENTES

But why Cienfuegos? Why the doctor?

ABUELA

They didn't like him.

FUENTES

But why?

ABUELA

Why, why, why – you talk like a parrot.

FUENTES

Are you the only one in town who speaks Spanish?

ABUELA

No.

FUENTES

Then why won't anyone talk to me?

ABUELA

They don't know you.

FUENTES

But you're talking to me –

ABUELA

It doesn't matter if I die. They've killed all my children.

FUENTES

Who killed them?

22

ABUELA

The men with guns.

FUENTES

But who are these men? Are they white or Indian?

ABUELA

When an Indian puts on a uniform he turns white.

A Man calls something from his window in an Indian dialect (don't translate).

You'd better go now, Doctor.

FUENTES

What's wrong?

ABUELA

The others don't know who you are.

FUENTES

I'm the man who taught your doctor. His name was Cienfuegos – he was a good student.

ABUELA

Cienfuegos wasn't a good doctor.

FUENTES

Why do you say that?

ABUELA

'Cause so many of his patients are dead!

She laughs dementedly. Fuentes looks at the sad village.

EXT. ROAD – DAY

Fuentes returns to his car. The window has been forced open. His suitcase is open on the ground. He finds his black bag undisturbed, but the camera is gone.

FUENTES

My camera! Dammit!

EXT. HOTEL – SIGN – NIGHT

Car headlights illuminate the sign of a hotel: 'POZO DE LOS CACIQUES' *over a painting of a naked Indian chief, knife in hand, about to sacrifice a maiden.*

INT. RESTAURANT – NIGHT

Andrew and Harriet sit at a table with another pair of Tourists.

> ANDREW
> (*English*)
> Thousands of them – tore their hearts out and threw them in the well. Must have had a labor surplus.

Harriet sees Fuentes passing through the dining room, looking tired.

> HARRIET
> (*English*)
> Hi! We meet again.

> ANDREW
> (*English*)
> The accounts say there was a stream of blood running down the pyramid.

> FUENTES
> (*don't translate*)
> Mexico.

> ANDREW
> (*English*)
> Pardon?

> FUENTES
> (*Spanish*)
> Not here. Maybe in Mexico. The Aztecs.

Andrew indicates his travel book.

> ANDREW
> (*English*)
> But it says here –

> FUENTES
> (*Spanish*)

Not our people. It was other tribes, attacking from the north.

Fuentes steps away.

> HARRIET
> (*English*)

Honey, he said it was foreigners from the north.

> ANDREW
> (*English*)

That's not what it says in the book.

EXT. POOL – NIGHT

A bug-zapper kills insects. Fuentes sits by the pool under the yellow lights, looking at his hands, thinking.

FLASHBACK: INT. CLASSROOM – DAY

Cienfuegos turns from something he is writing on the blackboard, smiles, turns back to his work.

> TOURIST WOMAN
> (*off-screen; English*)

I found this in the lobby.

> COMPANION
> (*off-screen; English*)

Go ahead, read it.

> TOURIST WOMAN
> (*off-screen; English*)

It's all in italics.

> COMPANION
> (*off-screen; English*)

So read it poetically.

EXT. POOL – NIGHT

Fuentes looks up. We pan with his gaze across to a pair of Americans sitting by the pool. The Tourist Woman reads from a travel brochure to her female Companion.

> TOURIST WOMAN
> (*English*)
> 'There is a place where the air is like a caress, where gentle waters flow, a place where your burdens are lifted from your shoulders on wings of peace –'

> COMPANION
> (*English*)
> They can't be talking about this place.

> TOURIST WOMAN
> (*English*)
> This is near Bali –
> (*resumes reading*)
> 'A place to forget, a place to grow, a place where each day is a gift and each person is reborn –'

CU: Fuentes leaning back to listen.

> (*off-screen; English*)
> 'Where is this paradise on earth, this haven, this safe harbor?'

FADE OUT

FADE IN:

INT. POLICE STATION – DAY

Fuentes sits in front of a Captain of the rural police.

> FUENTES
> They murdered Cienfuegos.

> CAPTAIN
> Who told you that?

> FUENTES
> I heard a rumor in the capital, I went to the village, and he wasn't there.

The Captain sighs, turns and sits at his desk.

26

CAPTAIN

He was kidnapped by guerrillas.

FUENTES

They told me he was burned to death.

CAPTAIN

What is your name, sir?

FUENTES

Doctor Fuentes. Humberto Fuentes.

The Captain writes Fuentes's name on a form.

CAPTAIN
(*don't translate*)

Doctor – Humberto – Fuentes – I'll send somebody to
investigate. We have to stop these rumors.

FUENTES

No, it won't make any difference – if the guerrillas kidnapped
him – killed him – then –

CAPTAIN

Then you'll be going home to the capital?

FUENTES

I'd like to keep going, visit one of my students in Tierra
Quemada.

CAPTAIN

I wouldn't advise you to go there.

FUENTES

Why not?

CAPTAIN

There have been incidents with guerrillas up there. Then
there are deserters, bandits. And the Indians, well, they're
Indians, right? They won't talk to anybody, they see a white
face and –

*He puts a finger to his lips to indicate silence. The Captain himself has
an Indian face.*

27

> FUENTES

I'm sure my student is there.

> CAPTAIN

Okay, but I can't guarantee your safety.

Fuentes shrugs his shoulders.

Could I see your identification? I need to be sure you're really a doctor and not a journalist. We've had problems with journalists. They go up to take pictures, then they disappear. And I get blamed for it.

Fuentes stands.

> FUENTES

I'm not taking any pictures. They stole my camera.

> CAPTAIN
> (*serious*)

Identification, please.

EXT. STREET – DAY

Fuentes steps out of the station and three young Boys run away. He sees that they've stolen his hub caps. One remains, spinning on the pavement.

EXT. RIVER COUNTRY – DAY

Fuentes drives through the beginning of hilly river country.

EXT. COUNTRYSIDE – DAY

Fuentes studies a map on the hood of his car, parked alongside the road in a hilly area. The Kokal truck blasts by, bottles clinking, horn honking.

Looking for Tierra Quemada on the map. Fuentes looks up at the hills.

There is a pathway, nearly covered with weeds, leading to the top of the nearest hill.

Fuentes considers, then takes his black bag from the station wagon. He begins to climb, passing through coffee plants growing haphazardly

along the trail. Suddenly there is a whistle. He stops, listening, then
continues.

EXT. TIERRA QUEMADA – DAY

A village even poorer than Rio Seco. Fuentes walks between the shacks.
There are no men, only Women, who turn their backs when he
approaches.

> FUENTES
> Excuse me, Señora. Do you know where Dr Arenas is? The
> doctor here. Do you know him, Señora? Dr Arenas. Nobody
> knows where Dr Arenas is? Dr Arenas. Don't you know him?
> Señoras, don't you know if he's here?

Once again, nobody will speak to him, suspicious. Finally a Young
Woman approaches with a Little Girl in her arms.

The Little Girl has a distended stomach. The Woman points to the
black bag and says something in an Indian language (don't translate).

Fuentes examines the child.

> She isn't sick. This is malnutrition and thirst. Food – what are
> you feeding her?

The Woman indicates her breasts.

> She's too big to be breast-feeding. She needs solid food. Like corn, understand?

MOTHER
There isn't any corn. Only coffee.

FUENTES
Then what do you eat?

MOTHER
Nothing.

She points at the black bag and speaks in her dialect (don't translate).

FUENTES
I don't have food, only medicine. Your child needs food. Vegetables, fruit, rice.

A boy of ten or eleven, Rabbit, has come closer, listening.

RABBIT
These are Coffee People. They pick coffee to buy food.

FUENTES
Okay, so buy food.

RABBIT
They say the coffee price is bad, so wages are too low to buy food. This village is fucked.

FUENTES
Where is the doctor? The other doctor, Dr Arenas?

RABBIT
He's gone.

FUENTES
Gone where?

RABBIT
They took him.

FUENTES
Who took him?

RABBIT

The Army.

FUENTES

Where?

RABBIT

To school.

FUENTES

Is he still there?

RABBIT

That's where they said they were taking him.

FUENTES

Where is the school?

Fuentes pulls out the map and points to a spot.

Look – we're here.

RABBIT

Here?

FUENTES

Here.

RABBIT

Really?

FUENTES

Yes. So where's the school?

Rabbit points.

Is there a road to get there?

RABBIT

For two reales I'll show you.

Fuentes sighs.

FUENTES

Okay, tell your mother you're coming with me.

                                    RABBIT

I don't have a mother.

                                    FUENTES

Your father?

                                    RABBIT

I don't have one.

                                    MOTHER

He doesn't have anyone.

The Mother watches Fuentes sigh, then leave with Rabbit.

EXT. ROAD – DAY

Rabbit sits down in the road. Fuentes turns when he notices.

                                    FUENTES

What's wrong?

                                    RABBIT

I'm hungry.
                              (*shrugs*)
I'm as fucked as the rest of them.

INT. STATION WAGON – DAY

Rabbit eats crackers while Fuentes drives.

                                    FUENTES

That woman needed food. That's who I should be feeding.

                                    RABBIT

She didn't have anything to sell.

Fuentes gives him a dirty look.

Here.

                                    FUENTES

What?

                                    RABBIT

Stop here.

Fuentes hits the brakes. There is nothing beside the road but woods.

FUENTES

The school is here?

RABBIT

No. But it's where the doctor is.

FUENTES

Show me.

RABBIT

I want my two reales first.

Fuentes gives him the money.

EXT. WOODS – DAY

The boy walks beside the doctor in the woods. They reach a clearing. At first Fuentes doesn't see what it is, but gradually he sees the human bones at his feet. They are walking in a secret cemetery.

FUENTES
(*surprised*)
These are people. Human beings.

RABBIT

Not any more.

FUENTES

What are they doing here?

RABBIT

This is where they take you when you graduate.

Fuentes picks up a piece of skull and looks at it. There is a bullet hole in the skull.

FUENTES

Why were they killed?

RABBIT

The Army was mad at them.

FUENTES

They didn't even bury them.

RABBIT

To make an example.

FUENTES

Example of what?

RABBIT

That it's a bad idea to get the Army mad at you.

FUENTES

And why did they kill Dr Arenas?

RABBIT

He was a doctor.

FUENTES

I know that, but why did they kill him?

RABBIT

Because he was a doctor.

Fuentes makes a face, drops a piece of skull.

FUENTES

Was he a good doctor?

RABBIT

Yes. When I broke my wrist he fixed it.

FUENTES

And the people in the village liked him?

RABBIT

No.

FUENTES

Why not?

RABBIT

He wasn't one of them.

FUENTES

People should know about this.

RABBIT

Everybody knows. The Army brought us to see what could happen.

FUENTES

I didn't know anything about it.

RABBIT

'Cause you're a stranger.

EXT. ROAD – AFTERNOON

Fuentes and Rabbit return to the station wagon.

FUENTES

I'll take you back.

RABBIT

Are you going home?

FUENTES

I don't know. Maybe I'll go on to Caras Sucias.

RABBIT

You'll get lost.

FUENTES

I know how to find it. You can't come with me.

RABBIT

Where are you going to sleep?

FUENTES

In a hotel.

RABBIT

There aren't any hotels out here.

FUENTES

And in your village?

RABBIT

They might kill you.

FUENTES

Who?

RABBIT

The men who are hiding. When you came there was a signal and all the men hid. Now that they know you're alone they might kill you.

FUENTES

I haven't done anything to them.

RABBIT

So what? You're a stranger. I know a place we can sleep.

EXT. SCHOOL – DUSK

The station wagon is parked in front of a ruined building at the edge of the woods.

INT. SCHOOL – DUSK

Broken desks and chairs, a blackboard covered with obscenities. We find Rabbit wandering amid the debris.

RABBIT

This used to be the school. When the teacher vanished the Army brought people in to question them. They'd scare you by saying, 'We're going to take you to school.' If you survived, people said you were 'educated.' If you didn't, they said you had 'graduated.'

FUENTES

How do you know all this?

Rabbit shrugs.

RABBIT

They took me with three girls. The girls washed their clothes and cooked and did it with them. And I did all the other work.

FUENTES

They were prostitutes?

RABBIT

The soldiers called them whores, but they didn't pay them.

FUENTES

These were white men?

RABBIT

The soldiers were all Indians. But the commander acted like he was white.

FUENTES

From where?

RABBIT

Not from here. They never send you to your own region.

Rabbit lies down on a long table with strips of leather attached to it.

I slept here.

Fuentes touches one of the leather thongs.

FUENTES

What are these for?

RABBIT

Operations.

FUENTES

They had a doctor?

RABBIT

They took your friend's tools after his 'education,' and used

37

them to make people talk. They call that 'operations.' The soldiers were always making jokes.

Rabbit opens the doctor's bag and pulls out a scalpel.

They used one of these.

FUENTES

Don't touch that!

Rabbit lies back down.

RABBIT

If you want to go to Caras Sucias tomorrow we have to start early. There isn't a path.

FUENTES

How can there be a village if there isn't a path?

RABBIT

They don't want to be found.

Fuentes sits on a wobbly chair. Rabbit closes his eyes.

The guys said they'd take me with them as a mascot, but the commander said no.
(*he looks to the doctor*)
I'll wake you at sunrise.

He closes his eyes again.

YOUNG GIRL
(*voice-over*)

The boy has no mother.

EXT. COOKFIRE – MORNING

We watch the hands of the Woman as she grinds corn into paste in a stone bowl, then slowly pan to see the Girl's hands as she inexpertly tries to pat corn mash into a tortilla.

MOTHER

His mother is alive but she won't look at him.

YOUNG GIRL

How can that be?

38

> **MOTHER**
> She was only a girl herself when soldiers came and forced her.
> The boy is something she pushed from her body. Use your
> fingertips.

> **YOUNG GIRL**
> How can he live?

> **MOTHER**
> As a dog lives. He takes the scraps that real people leave.

> **YOUNG GIRL**
> So he's bad?

> **MOTHER**
> Dogs can't be bad or good. They're just dogs.

EXT. CARAS SUCIAS − MORNING

Fuentes walks through ruins, followed by Rabbit.

*Caras Sucias is a deserted village at the edge of low tropical jungle.
Nothing much remains of the houses – burnt and tumbled-down.*

> **FUENTES**
> There's nobody left.

> **RABBIT**
> These were Banana People. They hid in the trees, but during
> Festival they got caught in the open and gunned down from a
> helicopter. The survivors have been taken away.

> **FUENTES**
> Why didn't you tell me?

> **RABBIT**
> You didn't ask me if there were people here.

> **FUENTES**
> Do you know what happened to the doctor here? Echevarria?

> **RABBIT**
> No.

FUENTES
(*angry*)
Okay – I'll take you back.

RABBIT
They don't want me there. They say I'm bad luck.

FUENTES
They're right.

RABBIT
You know how to find the main road?

Fuentes thinks. He doesn't know.

You know how to find Los Martires?

FUENTES
It's up higher.

RABBIT
You ever been there?

FUENTES
Have you?

Rabbit smiles.

EXT. ROAD – DAY

Fuentes and Rabbit look at the station wagon. The tires have been stolen.

FUENTES
Dammit. This fucking country.

The soda truck blasts past, going back toward the capital, the drivers honking and waving but not stopping.

Assholes!

EXT. ROAD – LATER

Fuentes and Rabbit wait. Rabbit is finishing the crackers. A thin young Indian man, Domingo, approaches on foot.

FUENTES
Señor! Did you see anybody with my tires?

Domingo doesn't answer.

Where are you coming from?

RABBIT
Watch it, mister. He's a soldier.

FUENTES
Do you speak Spanish? Did you see somebody with tires?
From my car –

Domingo steps right up to Fuentes and looks him in the eye. He acts
totally fearless compared with the other people Fuentes has encountered
in the villages.

DOMINGO
I don't know anything about your fucking tires. How much
money have you got?

Fuentes is terrified. Domingo grabs Rabbit.

Give me your money or I'll break his arm.

41

FUENTES

He isn't mine.

DOMINGO

So what?

RABBIT

I've only got two reales.

DOMINGO

Give them to me.

Rabbit gives his money to Domingo, who pushes him away and pulls a pistol from his pants. He waves it at the doctor.

And you?

Fuentes hands him his wallet. Domingo pulls the money out and tosses the wallet on the ground.

FUENTES

At least let me have the tires back.

DOMINGO

How could I have your tires? Somebody with a jack took them. Give me the keys.

Fuentes gives the keys to Domingo. Domingo opens the rear door, pulling out bottles of water. He opens the black bag and pulls out the scalpel.

What are you doing out here?

FUENTES

Visiting a friend.

DOMINGO

Where?

FUENTES

He works in Pico de Aguila.

DOMINGO

You can't reach that village by car.

Domingo takes the scalpel and the keys and a bottle of water and walks ahead up the road.

FUENTES

Some soldier.

DISSOLVE TO:

EXT. ROAD – NIGHT

Fuentes and Rabbit lie on the hood of the station wagon. We hear the insects singing.

RABBIT

If there's a battle and a soldier loses his rifle, the captain says he must be a spy, and the soldier is executed.

FUENTES

That's stupid.

RABBIT

They've got discipline. When I was their mascot I saw it lots of times. Maybe that's what happened to the man who took my money.

FUENTES

Two reales. I had hundreds in my wallet.

RABBIT

Do you have a house in the capital?

FUENTES

Yes.

RABBIT

And you have more money there?

FUENTES

It's in the bank.

RABBIT

Then what're you crying about? He took all I had in the world.

Fuentes scowls and looks down the empty road.

FUENTES

Nobody drives on this road.

RABBIT

Nobody but idiots.

Fuentes gives him a dirty look. The headlights of a car appear.

FUENTES

Somebody's coming.

RABBIT

Some idiot.

Fuentes gets up to signal. The car swerves very close, almost hitting him, then running off the road, skidding to a halt between the trees. Domingo steps out, wounded in the side.

FUENTES

Run away, kid!

Rabbit doesn't budge. Domingo staggers up with his pistol drawn.

Are you hurt?

Domingo points the gun at him.

DOMINGO

Put the tires onto your car.

44

Fuentes hesitates.

> FUENTES
>
> Where did you get it?

Rabbit passes Fuentes, heading for the car.

> I told you to run!

> DOMINGO
>
> Hurry up! There's a jack in the trunk.

Rabbit pulls a flashlight from the glove compartment. He flicks it on.

> RABBIT
>
> Tourists. Tourists always have flashlights.

He plays the light on Domingo's bleeding wound. Domingo is sweating heavily, in a lot of pain.

> DOMINGO
>
> Point it at the tires!

EXT. WOODS – NIGHT

Fuentes operates on Domingo as he lies on the ground between cars, their headlights on. Rabbit holds the flashlight. Domingo watches too, pointing his pistol at Fuentes, sweat covering his face.

> DOMINGO
>
> What are you doing? Tell me what you're doing!

> FUENTES
>
> The bullet went through your arm and lodged in your ribs. I have to give you a shot.

> DOMINGO
>
> Don't knock me out.

> FUENTES
>
> You can't take the pain.

> DOMINGO
>
> Just do it.

Fuentes cuts. Rabbit leans in to see the gory details.

EXT. ROAD – MORNING

Dawn. The station wagon has new tires.

Fuentes arranges his instruments while Rabbit wraps Domingo in a bandage. Domingo has a bad color.

> DOMINGO
> You don't have much experience with bullets.

> FUENTES
> My patients aren't thieves.

No reaction from Domingo.

> The boy said you're a deserter.

Domingo shoots a look at Rabbit.

> DOMINGO
> I was a medic in the Army. If they stop us, say I'm your driver and that I was bitten by a snake.

> FUENTES
> What?

> DOMINGO
> Say I was pissing at the side of the road and a snake bit me.

> FUENTES
> Where are we going?

> DOMINGO
> Further on. You'll drive. You can give me a shot for the pain. But not enough to knock me out.

Fuentes takes a small bottle from his bag.

> What is that? I can't read the label.

> FUENTES
> It's an analgesic.

Fuentes fills a hypodermic with liquid from the bottle.

DOMINGO
(*to Rabbit*)

Can you read?

RABBIT

No.

FUENTES

You have to trust me.

DOMINGO

What is it exactly?

FUENTES

You have to trust me.

Domingo grabs the syringe and points the pistol at Rabbit.

DOMINGO

Your pants.

FUENTES

He's just a boy!

DOMINGO

I'll give him half a dose and see what it does.
(*to Rabbit*)

Drop your pants!

RABBIT

First give me my two reales back.

DOMINGO

When I get where I'm going.

*Rabbit pulls his pants down. Fuentes watches, expressionless, Domingo
searching his eyes as he spikes the boy's buttock and injects the drug. He
pulls it out, watches Rabbit for a moment.*

RABBIT

What?

Domingo shoots himself up with the other half of the dose.

FUENTES

Where are we going?

47

DOMINGO

Further ahead. Let's go.

INT. STATION WAGON – AFTERNOON

Fuentes drives. Rabbit watches the countryside pass with clouded eyes. Domingo sits in back with his leg stretched out.

FUENTES

Did you kill the tourists?

DOMINGO

Who?

FUENTES

The ones whose tires we took. Did you kill them?

DOMINGO

No.

FUENTES

Why not?

DOMINGO

What do you care?

FUENTES

Who shot you?

DOMINGO

It doesn't matter.

Rabbit begins to talk in an Indian dialect. Domingo talks with him for a moment in the same language (don't translate).

FUENTES

What'd he say?

DOMINGO

He says he's never been in an airplane before.

EXT. ROAD – AFTERNOON

Fuentes and Domingo wait by the car as Rabbit vomits over the side of a bridge.

48

FUENTES

He won't run away.

Domingo gives him a look.

DOMINGO

Am I going to die from this?

FUENTES

Not if you get treatment.

DOMINGO

Then you'll get to live a little longer.

Rabbit comes back, wiping his mouth.

FUENTES

If you're going to get better you have to sleep.

DOMINGO

You first.

EXT. WOODS – NIGHT

The station wagon is parked in a clearing in the trees.

INT. STATION WAGON – NIGHT

Domingo and Rabbit sleep. Fuentes opens his eyes, watches Domingo for a moment. He reaches back slowly and lightly lifts the pistol from Domingo's hand. He opens the chamber, looks – no bullets. He smiles, closes the chamber and returns the pistol to Domingo.

EXT. MERCADO – LATE MORNING

The station wagon slows, people barely moving out of the way as they drive through the market of a small town – a stone church, plaza, stucco buildings painted in pastels. Things don't seem so desperate here.

INT. CAR – LATE MORNING

Domingo is in pain again, the drug worn off, and very nervous.

DOMINGO

Keep moving, dammit! I told you not to go this way!

> FUENTES

There's no way around this town.

> DOMINGO

What are you doing?

Fuentes pulls the car to the side when there is a spot free of vendors.

> FUENTES

We need food and water. Bring the money.

He is out of the car before Domingo can make another threat.

EXT. MARKET – LATE MORNING

Fuentes begins to stroll past the stalls and groundcloths, checking out the goods. Domingo lurches after him, wincing on the bad leg, and Rabbit wanders behind. They walk past a wall covered with stencils of various political parties and much graffiti, much of it spray-painted over. There is a partially vandalized poster of the General, exhorting the populace to be vigilant against subversives. Fuentes sees something, frowns, and stops in front of a Vendor sitting behind a blanket covered with cheap manufactured goods, just as Domingo catches up.

> FUENTES

Where did you get these things?

No response. Fuentes turns to Domingo.

Where are these from? Ask him.

Domingo gives him a dark look, but then translates Fuentes's question into the local Indian language. The Vendor answers (don't translate).

> DOMINGO

From the city.

Fuentes bends and lifts something off the Vendor's blanket.

CU: speculum. Fuentes lifts the shiny medical instrument.

> FUENTES
> (off-screen)

And he got this in the city too?

The Vendor nods in answer to Domingo's question (don't translate).

Ask him what it is.

Domingo asks (don't translate).

DOMINGO
He doesn't know.

FUENTES
Does he know what any of these are?

Fuentes indicates a group of medical instruments lying side by side on the blanket (don't translate).

DOMINGO
He says they're for a doctor. He'll give you a good price if you want them.

FUENTES
And where is the doctor's office? Dr de Soto?

Another exchange (don't translate).

DOMINGO
He says there is no doctor.

FUENTES
Tell him I know these are stolen. If he won't tell me where Dr de Soto is I'll bring the police.

The Vendor has a worried exchange with Domingo (don't translate).

DOMINGO
At the end of that street. But he says the doctor isn't there.

FUENTES
We'll see about that.

Fuentes starts away.

DOMINGO
Where are you going?

Fuentes walks away. Domingo struggles to catch up.

Seen from a distance, Fuentes is asking a soldier for directions. He turns and points back toward us. We shift to see Domingo in the foreground, ducking behind a building, sweat beading from his forehead.

INT. BARBER SHOP – DAY

Fuentes steps into a makeshift barber shop. The Barber is cutting the hair of a Client in front of a small mirror. All the furnishings of the room belong to a modest doctor's office – government hygiene posters still on the wall, a curtained partition and cot in one corner, a glass cabinet still holding a few bottles and boxes of medicine.

> BARBER

Good afternoon.

> FUENTES

Good afternoon. Is the doctor in?

The Barber and Client look at each other.

This is Dr de Soto's office?

> BARBER

It was.

> FUENTES

He's not here any more?

> CLIENT

The doctor has passed away.

Fuentes looks very tired. He indicates a chair.

> FUENTES

Do you mind if I sit?

> BARBER

Please, sit.

Fuentes sits, bends to hold his head in his hands.

> FUENTES

May I ask how the doctor died?

The Barber and Client look at each other again. The Barber sighs, crosses to pull the shade down on the window to the street. We see Domingo glaring in before it blocks our view of him. The Barber begins to speak quietly.

BARBER

It was very unfortunate. He was murdered by guerrillas.

FUENTES

Guerrillas came into this town?

CLIENT

How can you stop them? When the Army isn't here they come.

BARBER

They come to shop, to visit their friends.

FUENTES

But what did they have against Dr de Soto?

BARBER

He treated wounded soldiers when the Army came. Then the guerrillas come back to punish the people who helped them.

FUENTES

What if he refused to treat the soldiers?

CLIENT
(*smiles*)

You don't refuse men with guns.

BARBER

They killed him to make an example.

Fuentes stands.

FUENTES

So now you don't have a doctor.

BARBER
(*shrugs*)

It seems simpler that way. Would you like a haircut?

EXT. MARKET – DAY

Domingo and Rabbit wait by the blanket of an old Indian Man.

RABBIT

Does it hurt?

DOMINGO
Yes.

RABBIT
A lot?

DOMINGO
Shut up.

A Boy of about fifteen approaches, looking to see that no soldiers are near.

Have you got them?

The Boy hands something to Domingo. He hides it in his hand, then hands a bill to the boy, who hurries away.

CU: hand. Domingo opens his hand and we see three bullets in the palm.

Here they are, kid. The Father, the Son and the Holy Spirit.

He quickly pockets the bullets as he sees Fuentes coming back from the barber shop.

Let's go.

FUENTES
Fine.

DOMINGO
I'm not kidding.

FUENTES
Of course you're not.

INT. CAR – ROAD – DAY

Fuentes drives wordlessly, thoroughly depressed. Domingo sits in the rear with Rabbit, who is happily eating small bananas.

DOMINGO
The rich use the Army to push the Indians from the good land, so they'll starve. So the Indians go pick their coffee. The Indians come back with their pitiful wages and those leeches suck them dry.

We see a Man up ahead in the road, dressed in rags, waving his arms. Domingo pushes the pistol against the back of Fuentes's neck.

Don't stop.

Fuentes ignores the pistol and begins to slow down.

I'm warning you –

FUENTES
Go ahead and shoot. If the Army see you alone in this car they'll arrest you in a minute.

Fuentes stops the wagon. The waving man, Portillo, smiles and sits in front by the doctor.

Hello.

PORTILLO
Hello.

FUENTES
Where are you headed?

Portillo shrugs.

PORTILLO
Further on.

Fuentes starts the car. He gives a look to Portillo – a white man who looks a little crazy.

FUENTES
Are you lost?

PORTILLO
(*laughing*)
Yes. For a long time now.

DOMINGO
(*suspicious*)
Where do you live?

PORTILLO
Neither here nor there.

DOMINGO

What's your name?

PORTILLO

Padre Portillo. But these days people just call me 'The Ghost.'

FUENTES

You're a priest?

PORTILLO

Not anymore. I was when I came here. I taught the Indians religion through theater. Poeple love drama. But I was a bad actor – I stopped believing in my role and lost my faith.

FUENTES

That's a shame. A man should believe in something.

PORTILLO

You're religious?

FUENTES

No, I'm a doctor – a scientist. I believe in progress.

PORTILLO

Always moving ahead –

FUENTES

That's it . . .

PORTILLO

These days I just believe in moving. It doesn't matter which direction.

They ride in silence for a moment.

FUENTES

I have to admit my faith has been shaken in the last few days.

PORTILLO

I'm sorry for you.

Domingo has been staring at the newcomer with undisguised suspicion.

DOMINGO

So you got a village girl pregnant.

56

> PORTILLO
> (*smiles*)

Oh, no. Much worse than that.

> DOMINGO

You stole from the church.

> PORTILLO

There was nothing to steal. I was a very good priest, until I was tested.

> FUENTES

Tested?

> PORTILLO

I was tested, and I was weak.

> FUENTES
> (*digging*)

A priest without faith is like a soldier without a rifle.

Domingo scowls at him.

EXT. ROAD – DAY

An older Campesino struggles up a hill with a huge bundle of branches cut for firewood on his back. The road winds down the long hill behind him. The station wagon glides from the far background, finally passing us out of frame. We hold on the man, still walking.

EXT. ROADSIDE – EVENING

Domingo is watching Rabbit camouflage the car with palm fronds. They've pulled off the road for the night. Portillo squats with his back against a tree, thinking as he talks to Fuentes.

> FUENTES

You can never save a life. You make it longer, make it better, relieve pain – but everybody dies. I wanted to leave something in the world, something –

> PORTILLO

Eternal?

FUENTES

Something practical. Something to be passed on from person to person.

PORTILLO

I wanted to save souls, but how much better to save a life. I dreamed your life and you dreamed mine.

FUENTES

And both ended up a total failure.

PORTILLO

You can't feel responsible for these students. The world is a hard place –

FUENTES

I should have warned them.

PORTILLO

If you didn't know what the danger was, how could you warn them?

FUENTES

I should have known.

PORTILLO
(*considers*)

Maybe. Maybe innocence is a sin.

He looks back into the trees, lowers his voice slightly.

Your driver doesn't like me.

FUENTES

He isn't my driver. He's just somebody heading in the same direction.

PORTILLO

How far are you going?

FUENTES

Till I find my students.

Domingo limps back to them.

58

DOMINGO
You can stay with us tonight, but in the morning you leave.

PORTILLO
May God bless you.

Fuentes turns to step further into the trees.

DOMINGO
Where are you going?

FUENTES
To relieve myself, if it's alright with you.

PORTILLO
Watch out for snakes.

EXT. WOODS – EVENING

Fuentes stands peeing in the woods. He stares at a gummy substance rolling down the tree, then looks up.

Fuentes's POV: machete scars. The bark has been scarred in a criss-cross pattern. Chicle sap seethes out of the cuts. Fuentes's hand appears, fingers touching the sap.

Fuentes pulls his zipper shut, turns – two men flank him, both with machete in hand. He gasps, surprised. One of the men smiles shyly.

AMPARO
Welcome.

EXT. WOODS – CAMPFIRE – NIGHT

The travelers sit around a fire by a palm frond lean-to with Amparo and Javier, a pair of leathery chicleros. A cauldron of gum is cooking nearby, while rough blocks of the stuff are piled beneath the lean-to. Javier is cooking coffee in a battered tin pot.

JAVIER
We don't get many visitors.

FUENTES
Where are you from?

AMPARO

Gum People just go where the sap is running.

FUENTES

But where were you born?

AMPARO

On the coast.

JAVIER

In the mountains. But we live wherever the work is.

Javier pours coffee into metal cups for them.

AMPARO

Do you know any stories?

FUENTES

Stories?

Amparo smiles and indicates the jungle around them.

AMPARO

We don't get television out here.

FUENTES

People come to places like this to get away from television.

JAVIER

It's good to have a story at night. If you talk loud enough you can't hear the mosquitoes whine.

PORTILLO

I'll tell you a story.

They turn their attention to Portillo. He has a strange look on his face.

JAVIER

Is it a true story?

PORTILLO

It's a ghost story.

We begin to track in tight on a CU of Portillo.

There was a priest who came to a mountain village to teach the Bible. He used theater – put on plays with the children to bring the holy word. But it was the time when the Army was mad at the people. Because the priest helped the people he became their enemy too. Before the killing began there were threats – anonymous notes, things painted on the church. But the people begged him not to go.

Portillo smiles bitterly.

They thought if he stayed God would protect them.

DISSOLVE TO:

INT. VILLAGE CHURCH – DAY

We see several Indian Men prying boards away from a makeshift altar in a tiny cinder-block church.

> PORTILLO
> (*voice-over*)
> The Army burned Los Suenos, which was above the village, but the people there had all become Baptists. Then they burned El Chino, which was below the village.

EXT. VILLAGE – DAY

A man's hand charred into a claw is in the dirt in the foreground. A hut burns in the background, a bloody, fire-blacked Child toddles in between, screaming. Soldiers rush by, dragging a corpse by the feet.

> PORTILLO
> (*voice-over*)
> In El Chino they were all Catholics.

INT. CHURCH ALTAR – DAY

We see the faces of the Men appear above us as the hole they are making widens.

> PORTILLO
> (*voice-over*)
> There was nothing bad or unusual happening in their village – they were just Corn People, working the land, having children, trying to feed them. Nobody was interested in politics.

The Men help Portillo out of his hiding place.

So when the Army came all they could think to do was hide.

CU: Portillo looking around at the Men. He is very frightened.

POV: Men looking at him with grim faces.

EXT. VILLAGE – DAY

The Men of the village sit on the ground in a circle, the Women and Children ringed around them. They are debating what to do.

> MOISES
> The Commandante left us this list of five men – five men and our Padre.

He nods toward Portillo, who sits among the Men.

These are the men he says we must execute.

> ISIDRO
> What have they done?

> GONZALO
> He says they are subversives. That they help the guerrillas.

JUNIPERO

That isn't true.

MOISES

The Commandante says it is. And he has men with guns. You saw them.

SIXTO

Can we fight them?

ISIDRO

With machetes? With hoes?

GONZALO

He says it is our duty to march the traitors to our cemetery, to dig holes, to kill them and leave them there till he returns.

CU: Portillo, terrified as he listens.

MOISES

If we fail to do this, he says he'll know we are bad people. His soldiers will burn our village and kill us all, like in El Chino and Los Suenos.

Villagers consider their limited options.

ARTEMIO

What if we run?

ISIDRO

If we run they will kill us in small groups instead of all together.

The Men think about this for a moment.

MOISES

We should have a vote on this.

GONZALO

We have three choices: try to fight and be slaughtered; try to run and be slaughtered; or sacrifice the men on the Commandante's list.

MOISES

May I see the hands of those who wish to fight?

Nobody raises a hand.

And those who wish to run?

Not a hand.

Those who think we must do as the Commandante tells us?

The Men resignedly raise their hands.

Portillo, in a kind of shock, hasn't moved.

(*off-screen*)
Father? Father?

Portillo snaps to, looks to Moises.

You haven't voted.

PORTILLO
I'm sorry. I vote with the majority.

The village head man nods gravely. Moises raises the list.

MOISES
Thank you. On the list are Padre Portillo, Isidro Mendez,
Jacobo Duran, Eufemio Ramirez, Sixto Lima, and I, Moises
Ibarra, am the sixth. These men have an hour to be with their
families and then we'll all meet at the cemetery.

He looks around to see if there are any objections.

It's best if we do this as quickly as possible.

*The Villagers rise slowly, without a word, and head back to their
dwellings. Portillo, still stunned, remains sitting.*

INT. CHURCH – STATUE

A crudely painted statue of Saint Sebastian, pin-cushioned with arrows.

Portillo knees at the altar, praying.

PORTILLO
(*voice-over*)
As a boy, the priest read the histories of the Christian martyrs
as if they were comic books. He often imagined his heroic
death at the hands of the infidels.

CU: Portillo, his mind working, trying to figure a way out of this.

   – a golden ray of light lifting him to the heavens, his soul resting at the right hand of God –

His eyes flick to the base of the altar.

The planks have not been replaced. His old hiding place beckons.

   – but when the reality was upon him, well –

EXT. VILLAGE – DAY

Portillo steps out of the tiny church and looks around. Not a soul in sight. He begins to walk, looking neither left nor right.

> PORTILLO
> (*voice-over*)
> The Church called the gospel he taught liberation theology. But he chose to liberate himself.

EXT. CEMETERY – DAY

We shoot past simple crosses and painted statues in the foreground and at Portillo as he reaches the edge of the village.

EXT. CORNFIELD – DAY

Portillo comes at us down an aisle of corn stalks.

> PORTILLO
> (*voice-over*)
> He knew the people of the village. He had eaten in their homes, shared their work, baptized their babies.

We track back when he reaches a CU.

> Because he knew them so well, he could imagine every detail of what would happen next.

EXT. CEMETERY – DAY

CU: shovel chops into the hard dirt of the cemetery.

The entire village, but for the priest, have gathered. Men take turns digging holes.

CU: chalice. Calloused fingers lift a communion wafer from the chalice and hold it aloft.

> **PORTILLO**
> (*voice-over*)
> Gonzalo, the sacristan, led the Christian part of the ceremony.

Muttering phrases, Gonzalo makes a sign of the cross in the air with the host.

> The priest's absence was noted by all, but nobody spoke of it.

Moises, kneeling, raises his chin to receive the sacrament.

> Their only hope was that the Commandante wouldn't blame them for his lack of faith. And so it went.

Moises swallows the wafer, then closes his eyes. The barrel of an old pistol is pressed to his forehead.

The hammer of the pistol begins to move forward – blam! The screen goes white.

FADE UP TO:

Overhead shot of graves.

We crane over the bodies lying dead on their backs in their freshly dug pits, foreheads bearing a blue-black hole – Moises, Isidro, Eufemio, Sixto, Jacobo. The last pit is empty.

> PORTILLO
> (*voice-over*)
> They could have sent someone to bring him back if they wanted to, but they didn't. I suppose they had their reasons.

Women lay stripped corn stalks across the pits, then begin to cover them with palm fronds as the rest of the villagers remain on their knees, praying.

They waited for the Commandante.

EXT. CHICLERO'S CAMP – NIGHT

The men ponder the story.

> PORTILLO
> Patience. The villagers clear a section of jungle knowing it will take seven, eight years for a decent yield. Do you know anybody with that kind of patience?

> FUENTES
> What happened to the village?

> PORTILLO
> I've been to the place where it was.

> FUENTES
> They were killed?

Portillo thinks a long time before answering.

> PORTILLO
> (*smiles sadly*)
> Obviously I don't believe in Heaven. But Hell – I can give you a tour of Hell.

> DOMINGO
> And the priest?

PORTILLO

I told you it was a ghost story. The priest wanders the roads
and pathways of the country, never sleeping in the same
place. He is neither here nor there – a ghost.

Silence as the men think. The fire pops.

AMPARO

I would hate to meet a ghost like that.

PORTILLO

What would you do if you were in the same situation?

AMPARO

If it was me? Who knows? I'm not a priest. Priests are not
regular people.

PORTILLO
(*smiles sadly*)
No. They're not supposed to be.

EXT. CAMP – NIGHT

*Once again Fuentes can't sleep. He rises and steps past the bodies of the
others.*

*A colorful tree frog is illuminated by a flashlight beam. Fuentes appears,
looking at the frog.*

INT. STATION WAGON – NIGHT

*Fuentes slips into the front seat of the car as quietly as he can. He
reaches over to the glove compartment, pulls out a photograph.*

*CU: photograph of Fuentes and his students in the class picture. He
covers the faces of the ones he knows are dead with his fingers. He
hovers a finger over Brazos, then covers him as well.*

FADE OUT

FADE UP TO:

EXT. ROADSIDE – SUNRISE

Domingo shifts a palm frond to see Fuentes asleep in the front seat of the car. We follow as he moves to the edge of the road, where Portillo stands shivering, watching the sun come up. Domingo watches him for a moment, then speaks softly.

DOMINGO
Could you hear my confession?

PORTILLO
I'm not a priest anymore. I don't wear a cassock anymore. See?

DOMINGO
I was a soldier and now I don't wear a uniform. Does that mean I haven't killed anyone?

PORTILLO
Killing the enemy in battle isn't the same as murder.

Domingo smiles bitterly, then squats at the side of the road, turning his face away from Portillo.

DOMINGO
It has been a long time since my last confession. Bless me, Father, for I have sinned.

CU: Domingo, as he continues his confession we lose his voice and hear Men's voices shouting.

EXT. ARMY CAMP – DAY

We see Soldiers ringed above us, shouting.

SOLDIERS
Do it! Give it to him! Do it!

Domingo stands in a pit below the Soldiers, in uniform, looking young and lost with a huge knife in his hand. We tilt to see an Indian Teenager, looking much like Domingo, lying on the ground at the bottom of the pit. The boy is wounded, bullet holes in his knees and chest.

Do it! Don't be a faggot! Give it to him!

Domingo's fingers tighten around the handle of the knife.

CU: Boy, lying on his back, looking up at Domingo with glassy eyes.

Domingo gets on his knees, holds the knife in both hands, then stabs hard and quick into the Boy's chest four times, blood spattering his face and arms. We hear applause of the Soldiers.

DISSOLVE TO:

EXT. ROADSIDE – MORNING

CU: Domingo, sad in his recollection.

> DOMINGO
>
> That was only the first. My initiation.

> PORTILLO
>
> I'm not a priest. I can't absolve you –

> DOMINGO
>
> Then what good are you? I ought to kill you.

Portillo holds his eyes for a long moment.

> PORTILLO
>
> As you wish.

INT. STATION WAGON – DAY

Fuentes driving, Portillo in front with him.

> FUENTES
>
> Tell me, Father, are sins only things that you do? Or can they be something that you don't do?

> PORTILLO
>
> There are sins of commission and sins of omission. And there is Original Sin. We are all born guilty in the eyes of the Lord.

> FUENTES
>
> If a man has hurt someone without wanting to – if there was no intention –

> PORTILLO
>
> He probably isn't a sinner.

> DOMINGO
>
> But he's an idiot, for sure.

Portillo turns to regard Domingo.

70

> PORTILLO

Of course. An idiot or a coward. If God kept such people
from heaven he would be very lonely.

They have started down a very steep hill, gaining on a truck.

> DOMINGO

Oh shit – Oh shit –

*The truck is military transport, the back chock full of young Soldiers
carrying rifles. The Soldiers stare back at the station wagon full of men.*

Pass them, dammit!

> FUENTES

It's too narrow.

> DOMINGO

Pass them!

Domingo is sweating again, nervous about the soldiers.

> PORTILLO

Are you in such a hurry?

Domingo reaches in his shirt to show Portillo his pistol.

> DOMINGO

You shut up.

> PORTILLO
> (*smiles*)

As you wish.

Fuentes mashes the gas pedal.

> FUENTES

Hang on.

EXT. TRUCK/STATION WAGON – DAY

*Fuentes tries to pass on the narrow, winding mountain road. The
Soldiers think it is funny, leaning to look over the side as the wagon
nearly hits the side of the truck, falls back, then revs forward for another
try. They cheer as the car finally scoots past.*

INT. CAR – DAY

Rabbit is exhilarated, Fuentes grimly satisfied.

RABBIT

What a ride!

FUENTES

Are you happy now?

DOMINGO

Shit! Shit!

Fuentes turns to see as they reach the bottom of the hill.

POV: Barricade. Fuentes sees a barricade up ahead, with armed Soldiers waiting around it. Domingo sees it as well.

Careful what you say, Doctor.

Fuentes slows, the troop truck catching up behind them. A Guard signals for them to stop and Soldiers surround the station wagon, rifles pointed. A Sergeant sticks his face in the window.

SERGEANT

Your identification.

Fuentes gives him his license. The Sergeant looks at it.

Doctor Fuentes –

FUENTES

That's right.

SERGEANT

And the others?

There is no way Domingo can do anything to stop Fuentes from turning him in and he knows it. He looks straight ahead, awaiting the verdict. When Fuentes hesitates, Portillo speaks up –

PORTILLO

This is his driver, and his son.

This brings the Sergeant's attention to Portillo.

> SERGEANT

And you?

> PORTILLO

A ghost.

The Sergeant doesn't see the humor in this.

The doctor was kind enough to pick me up in the middle of nowhere.

The Sergeant waggles his finger at Portillo.

> SERGEANT

You come with me.

Portillo looks back to give Domingo a little smile as he gets out.

> PORTILLO

I absolve you.

The Soldiers take Portillo to their interrogation shack. The Sergeant points Fuentes toward the path to the left.

> SERGEANT

Stop when you reach the town.

They watch as Portillo is taken away.

> FUENTES

Why'd he do that?

> DOMINGO

He's crazy. And he's a lousy priest.

EXT. MODELO. DAY

Fuentes, Domingo and Rabbit come to a sign hanging over the entrance to a fenced-in refugee camp. The sign says: 'MODELO #4 – COMMUNITY OF HOPE.' It is not a town but a wire and cement prison. Rows of identical shacks with corrugated metal roofs surrounded by barbed wire. A pair of bored Soldiers signal for Fuentes to stop. The Indian Inhabitants look without expression from in front of their hovels.

> RABBIT

They bring the people in here after they burn their villages.

FUENTES

Why?

RABBIT

To protect them.

FUENTES

Protect them? From what?

RABBIT

From the guerrillas.

FUENTES

They're afraid of the guerrillas?

DOMINGO

They're country people. They're afraid of everything. The Army thinks they'll help the guerrillas if they don't watch them all the time.

EXT. MODELO – DAY

We track past a line of Indians waiting for the doctor's help. We reach a table where Fuentes is examining the villagers under the gaze of the Sergeant. Domingo sits a few yards away, talking to the people in the line, as he expertly applies a dressing to the ulcerated leg of a Little Boy.

SERGEANT

Our doctor only comes every three months.

FUENTES

Wasn't there a doctor in Pico de Aguila before you got here? Doctor Hidalgo?

SERGEANT

He was executed.

Fuentes is no longer surprised.

It was almost a year ago.

FUENTES

Why?

SERGEANT

For helping the guerrillas.

FUENTES

You're sure of that?

SERGEANT

What other reason would an educated man live out here?

FUENTES

Maybe he just wanted to help the Indians.

SERGEANT

It's the same thing.

(*suspicious*)

How come your driver wasn't driving?

Fuentes thinks for a moment, decides.

FUENTES

A snake bit him. He took a leak in the bushes and a snake bit him.

The Sergeant laughs.

SERGEANT

That'll teach him to hold his water.

EXT. SHACK – DAY

Rabbit is in front of a shack in another part of the town with a pair of Kids about his age, kicking a ragged soccer ball around.

KID

It's much further on, up in the high jungle. They call it Cerca del Cielo.

RABBIT

Fairy tales.

KID

Everybody says it's true.

RABBIT

Has anybody ever come back from there?

KID

Why would anybody come back to Modelo?

EXT. MODELO – DAY

Fuentes is treating ulcers in the mouth of a Little Girl sitting on the table. The Sergeant is gone. Domingo comes over next to him, limping slightly, trying to hide the pain in his leg.

FUENTES

You should rest that.

DOMINGO

If that priest sings I'm fucked.

Fuentes nods to indicate the Sergeant who is watching them from across the way.

FUENTES

Help me with these people. Ask them what their problems are. I don't understand this dialect.

Domingo checks out the Little Girl's mouth, asking her what the problem is in Indian (don't translate).

DOMINGO

She's got ulcers.

FUENTES

What color?

DOMINGO

White.

Fuentes grabs a bottle of pills.

FUENTES

It's a virus. You treat it with this. Three pills a day for two weeks.

Domingo gives the instructions to the Mother, who thanks him and takes her daughter away (don't translate).

How many years were you in the Army?

DOMINGO

Two. You treat a lot of skin rashes, dysentery, now and then
somebody gets shot.

FUENTES

You operated?

DOMINGO

Only if there wasn't a doctor there. Sometimes they died,
sometimes they didn't.
(*shrugs*)
We never had much medicine. The officers always sold it.

Rabbit rejoins them, breathless.

RABBIT

I got the whole story. The people are from Pico de Aguila.
They brought them here and then burned the town. Your
friend Hidalgo is dead.

FUENTES

The Sergeant told me.

RABBIT

The people say there's a village further on. It's so high and so
hidden the Army has never been able to find it. They call it
Cerca del Cielo.

DOMINGO

There's always rumors like that.

RABBIT

They say the refugees from the burnt villages have gone there
to hide. They say there's a young doctor who lives there, a
doctor named –

FUENTES

Montoya?

RABBIT

Yes. That's it.

FUENTES
(*sighs*)

She's the last one.

77

The next in line is a young woman, Graciela, looking apprehensive. An old woman, Vieja, stands behind her.

Come forward.

Graciela hesitates.

Closer.

She won't budge.

(*to Domingo*)
Ask what her problem is.

Domingo just looks away. Fuentes turns to Rabbit.

You.

Rabbit repeats the question in Indian, and Vieja answers him in the same language (don't translate).

RABBIT
The old woman says this girl's stomach hurts.

FUENTES
Since when?

Another exchange between Rabbit and Vieja (don't translate).

RABBIT
Since she was raped by soldiers. She hasn't spoken a word since that day.

FUENTES
When was that?

RABBIT
Two years ago.

FUENTES
Then the problem is in her mind.

DOMINGO
Give her a pill.

FUENTES
I can't cure imaginary diseases. I'm not a psychologist.

Domingo grabs a card of aspirin tablets and holds them out to Graciela, not looking in her eyes.

> DOMINGO
>
> Take these.

The old woman nods her thanks.

> VIEJA
>
> May God bless you.

EXT. MODELO – NIGHT

A Soldier watches from his sentry box.

EXT. BARRACKS BUILDING – NIGHT

Rabbit stands in the midst of a group of Children staring through a window. We hear machine-gun fire.

Children's POV: Soldiers, TV.

A dozen Soldiers sit inside on folding chairs watching a Rambo*-type movie on a VCR.*

Rabbit is rapt. Domingo appears beside him.

> DOMINGO
>
> If you want to come it has to be now.

Rabbit gives a longing glance back at the TV as they step away.

EXT. STATION WAGON – NIGHT

Fuentes, Domingo and Rabbit sit in the car. The Sergeant gives Fuentes back his license.

> SERGEANT
>
> You'd better head back to the capital. We have word that there are guerrillas operating around here. They stole some tourists' car.

> FUENTES
>
> What happened to the man who was with us?

SERGEANT
(*shrugs*)
You shouldn't be picking people up off the road. On your
way.

EXT. ROAD – NIGHT

The station wagon cruises toward us slowly.

INT. CAR – NIGHT

Domingo sits in front with Fuentes.

DOMINGO
Why didn't you turn me in when you had the chance?

FUENTES
I should have. I'm a bad citizen.

Domingo considers this.

DOMINGO
You won't find her. There's nothing up there.

Fuentes brakes as he sees something ahead.

Their POV: Graciela.

*Graciela appears in the headlights, standing in the middle of the road.
Fuentes stops.*

INT./EXT. STATION WAGON – NIGHT

They look at the mute girl through the windshield.

DOMINGO
Go around her.

*Fuentes gives him a dirty look and steps out of the car. Rabbit steps up
behind him.*

FUENTES
What are you doing out here?

*Graciela just stands there. Rabbit says something in Indian (don't
translate) and she nods, pointing away and upward.*

> RABBIT

She wants to go to Cerca del Cielo.

> FUENTES

We don't know where it is.

Rabbit gives Fuentes a challenging look.

> RABBIT

So?

Fuentes sighs, waves her over.

INT. STATION WAGON – NIGHT

Domingo glares at Fuentes as Graciela gets in the back with Rabbit.

> DOMINGO

We should start charging bus fare.

INT. RUINED CHURCH – NIGHT

Fuentes, Domingo, Rabbit sit warming themselves by a little campfire they've made inside a burnt-out church. Graciela sits apart from them, in the shadows. We hear water flowing nearby.

FUENTES

You'll be warmer if you come next to the fire.

Graciela doesn't answer, watching them without expression.

CU: Graciela. Her eyes go down, she sits.

Her POV: pistol on the floor next to Domingo.

Graciela looks up at Domingo's face.

RABBIT
(*off-screen*)

She's afraid of us.

On the fire and men.

FUENTES

Then why did she come?

RABBIT

She's more afraid of the soldiers at Modelo.

Fuentes scowls and looks around.

FUENTES

So this is what's left of Pico.

RABBIT

I think Pico is behind us now. This is some other place.

DOMINGO

Another place where everybody is dead.

RABBIT

Or gone to Cerca del Cielo.

DOMINGO

There is no such place.

RABBIT

How do you know?

CU: Graciela curls herself in a ball on her blanket on the floor, her back to the conversation. She listens intently as Domingo tries to deflate the idea of a free town.

                    DOMINGO

When I was in the Army they always talked about this place.
But we never found it.

                     RABBIT

So it's really well hidden.

                    DOMINGO

We never found it because it doesn't exist. We even searched
in helicopters. If people have cleared land to plant we would
have seen it from the air. If they haven't, then they've starved.

                     RABBIT

Just because you haven't seen it, doesn't mean it's not there.

                    DOMINGO

You can believe in Heaven if you want, kid. See where it gets
you.

                    FUENTES

So why are you coming with us?

                    DOMINGO
                    (shrugs)

Where else can I go?

EXT. RUINED CHURCH – EARLY MORNING

The rising sun hits the side of the church.

INT. CHURCH – MORNING

*CU: pistol. Once again the pistol lies a few inches from Domingo's hand
as he sleeps. This time it is Graciela who steals it.*

Fuentes's eyes open as we see Graciela's feet pass by.

EXT. TREES/RIVERSIDE – MORNING

*Fuentes moves through the trees, trying to find where the girl has gone.
He comes out by the water, freezes. Graciela sits on the bank of a
beautiful lagoon-like wide spot in the river with the pistol aimed at her
forehead, with her thumb inside the trigger guard.*

FUENTES
(*softly*)

Señorita –

Graciela stiffens, but doesn't shoot and doesn't turn. Fuentes thinks the gun is still unloaded, and speaks very off-handedly.
If you shoot yourself now, you'll wake the others up.

Graciela's thumb stiffens on the trigger.

I mean if you want, be my guest, but it seems like a waste when we're almost to Cerca del Cielo.

Graciela doesn't budge, but she's listening.

I know Domingo said it doesn't exist but he's just bitter. He's been disappointed so often. He's lost all hope.

Graciela is crying, her hands starting to shake. Fuentes thinks, remembering, as he approaches. He speaks gently.

Cerca del Cielo is a very special place. A place where the air is like a caress, where gentle waters flow, a place where your burdens are lifted from your shoulders on wings of peace. A place to forget, a place where each day is a gift and each person is reborn.

CU: Graciela. She lowers the gun, her hands shaking.

And it's not very far from here. Just a little bit further on.

She turns to look at him. Fuentes picks up the gun, snorts his disapproval then holds it to his own temple.

Right –

He is about to pull the trigger when Domingo hollers.

Fuentes looks amused, lowers the gun.

He hates it when people play with his things.

Domingo crashes out on the bank above them, freezing when Fuentes turns and points the gun at him.

> DOMINGO
> Shit.

Fuentes gets up and tosses the pistol to him. He catches it, terrified it will go off.

> FUENTES
> Let's go.

EXT. ROAD – DAY

CU: pistol tucked snugly back in Domingo's pants.

Wider: the passengers are all out standing in front of the station wagon looking up. We pan with their gaze – the road stops at the foot of a mountain.

> FUENTES
> There's no path.

EXT. MOUNTAIN – DAY

They climb through the jungle vegetation, Rabbit in the lead. Fuentes breathes with difficulty, Domingo limping at the rear.

Domingo looks ahead at Graciela. She climbs solemnly. We zoom in on Domingo.

DISSOLVE TO:

EXT. VILLAGE – DAY

Burnt houses, shots ringing out, Woman screaming and crying. We follow the legs of an Indian Girl as she is dragged toward a hut. We tilt to see Domingo, in uniform, lagging behind the Soldiers who are dragging the Girl away. One of his fellow Soldiers pushes him into the hut after the Girl and the Men.

SOLDIER

Hurry up! You got to get it while they're still fresh!

INT. HUT – INDIAN GIRL – DAY

She's only thirteen or fourteen. She looks at the ceiling, eyes filled with tears.

Domingo leans over her.

INDIAN GIRL

Don't do it! Don't do it!

His shadow covers her face.

EXT. MOUNTAIN – DAY

Domingo is fighting the memory. Fuentes stops ahead, gasping for breath.

DOMINGO

Keep going.

FUENTES

I have to rest.

Domingo points the gun.

DOMINGO

Move it!

FUENTES

Go ahead. Shoot.

Domingo glares at him.

DOMINGO

Fuck it.

He climbs up away from them.

FUENTES

You're going to get that wound infected!

Fuentes sits. Rabbit sits by him and Graciela waits nearby. Fuentes looks around at the tangled jungle vegetation.

Human beings can't survive in this. Jaguars, snakes, insects that eat everything in sight.

RABBIT

You have to burn it all away and start from scratch.

FUENTES

But why come here in the first place?

RABBIT

To get away from white people.

FUENTES
(*laughing*)
I guess that might be worth it. There should be somewhere that white people aren't allowed.

ANDREW
(*off-screen; English*)

Helloooooooo!

Fuentes and Rabbit exchange a look. The doctor moves to the left a few yards, walking through the trees till he steps into a clearing in the jungle – a clearing filled with ancient stone ruins. Andrew and Harriet are on the stairs of a pyramid in the distance, waving.

EXT. RUINS – DAY

We see the ruins of an ancient city. The jungle around it seems to reclaim the clearing.

ANDREW
(*off-screen; English*)
It's a unique mixture of architectures –

Fuentes walks with the tourists, Rabbit and Graciela lagging behind.

HARRIET
(*English*)
You wouldn't believe –

ANDREW
(*English*)
It isn't clear yet if the Lotecs were a homogeneous group or a mongrelized culture –

HARRIET
(*English*)
– what we've been through –

ANDREW
(*English*)
Most of the evidence suggests they were driven up here by the more dominant civilizations.

HARRIET
(*English*)
A man stole our car punta de pistola! Like in *Treasure of the Sierra Madre*! The police found the car, but no *llantas* – tires? *Llantas*? Yeah, sí? Not one.

ANDREW
(*English*)
Another theory is that this site was founded by runaways from different cities in the lowlands. Possibly people earmarked for sacrifice.

FUENTES
(*Spanish*)
Americans are obsessed by these sacrifices.

HARRIET
(*English*)
Oh, *verdad*. Honey, he says we're hung up on sacrifice.

>   ANDREW
>   (*English*)
> Well, the concept of sacrifice is a tough one to sell in the
> States. You know – you don't look so good, Doctor. This is
> the Tropics – you've got to watch yourself.

>   HARRIET
>   (*English*)
> You okay?

EXT. RUINS – DAY

*CU: picnic. A cloth spread on the ground, covered with bread, wine,
cheese, fruit.*

Fuentes, Rabbit and Graciela sit with the tourists.

>   ANDREW
>   (*English*)
> They were gone before the Spanish got here. Fell apart on
> their own. Civil war, family feuds –

>   FUENTES
>   (*Spanish*)
> Like Europe at the same time –

>   HARRIET
>   (*don't translate*)
> Oh, sí – Europa –

>   ANDREW
>   (*English*)
> Europe was in much worse shape. *Mas peor?* Europe bit the
> big one. Here at least there was some organization, some
> pattern to the killing. Some meaning. In Europe it was all
> warlords, feudal disputes, little ethnic conflicts –

>   HARRIET
>   (*English*)
> It is so peaceful here. *Como tranquilo?*

89

ANDREW
(*English*)

They battled the jungle to carve out a living for themselves. Incas, Aztecs, Olmecs, Toltecs, Zapotecs –

FUENTES
(*Spanish*)

And here?

ANDREW
(*English*)

Here? Here the jungle won.

At the edge of clearing Harriet and Andrew, backpacks strapped on, say goodbye to Fuentes.

FUENTES
(*Spanish*)

Are you sure you'll be alright?

HARRIET
(*English*)

Don't worry – Andrew has a magnificent sense of direction.

ANDREW
(*English*)

We'll probably see you at the hotel at Tres Cruces.

FUENTES
(*Spanish*)

Yes. Probably.

EXT. PYRAMID – DUSK

The sun sets behind the crest of the pyramid.

Fuentes sits on the flat rocks in front of the pyramid, watching Rabbit and Graciela finish the food the tourists left.

RABBIT

I was a guide at the ruins at Xtal. The gringos gave me bigger tips if I made up bloody stories. I told them the priests ripped the hearts from virgins, then ate them.

FUENTES
It's going to be cold here tonight. I must be going crazy –

There is a sound. Domingo steps into the clearing, his hands tied behind his back, looking scared. Blood has soaked through his socks where he was wounded. Four Guerrillas step out behind him.

GUERRILLA I
Good evening.

The men fan out to surround them, looking around the ruins to be sure they are alone.

You're visiting the ruins?

FUENTES
We were just resting here.

GUERRILLA I
(*points to Domingo*)
Do you know this man?

Domingo pleads with his eyes.

FUENTES

Yes.

GUERRILLA I

He says he escaped from Modelo and the soldiers shot him.
He says you found him on the road and treated his wound.

FUENTES

That's true.

The Guerrilla holds out a pistol.

GUERRILLA I

Where did he get this?

FUENTES

He must have stolen it.

The Guerrilla nods, jams the gun into his belt.

GUERRILLA I

I wish he'd stolen more than three bullets.

Fuentes gives Domingo a look. Three bullets?

Untie him.

*One of the others unties Domingo. The Guerrilla Leader sits by Fuentes
on the rock.*

So what are you really doing here?

FUENTES

I'm looking for a friend, Dr Montoya. They told me she's fled
to these mountains, living with refugees.

GUERRILLA 2

Dr Montoya is at Cerca del Cielo.

FUENTES

You're sure?

GUERRILLA 2

The Army tried to kill her, but she got away and went up
there. That's what everybody says.

FUENTES

Where is it?

GUERRILLA 1

We can't tell you.

FUENTES

She's my friend, my student –

GUERRILLA 2

We don't know where it is. This village – Cerca del Cielo –
we've never seen it.

GUERRILLA 1

Maybe it's only a rumor. Like the story about Dr Montoya.

GUERRILLA 2

Whenever we go looking for it we keep circling back to this
place.

(*points*)

Is there any more food?

FUENTES

Please – help yourselves.

*The Guerrillas sit to eat. Graciela moves away, watching them
fearfully. The Leader struggles to pull his boot and sock off.*

GUERRILLA 1

You people should go home. It's dangerous in these
mountains.

He lifts a sore-looking foot.

Hey – do you have anything for blisters?

INT. AUTOPSY ROOM – DAY

*We pan around the faces of the Medical Students, eyes grave over their
surgical masks, looking down at a corpse they are dissecting. The corpse
is a small Indian Girl, probably a street kid. We come to Fuentes, doing
the actual cutting in the Girl's chest. He glances over at something.*

*Fuentes's POV: long, silky black hair slides over the rubber-gloved
fingers of one of the Students. We tilt up to see Montoya, a serious*

*young woman, contemplating death at close range. She senses Fuentes
watching her, looks up to him, embarrassed, then lets the little Girl's
hair drop and looks back to her chest cavity.*

> GUERRILLA 2
> (*off-screen*)

They do have it.

> GUERRILLA 3
> (*off-screen*)

No they don't.

> GUERRILLA 2
> (*off-screen*)

What do you know?

EXT. RUINS – NIGHT

The moon hangs over the trees surrounding the pyramid.

> GUERRILLA 3
> (*off-screen*)

They don't have it. Why should I believe you? Let's ask the
doctor – he should know.

*The group is arranged by the fire, lying on blankets. Fuentes is still
awake, as are the two youngest of the Guerrillas, boys in their early
teens.*

> GUERRILLA 2

Sir?

> FUENTES

Yes?

> GUERRILLA 2

You're from the city?

> FUENTES

That's right.

> GUERRILLA 2

Do you know the ice-cream store across from the bus station?

FUENTES

I used to take my daughter there.

GUERRILLA 2

What are the flavors they sell?

FUENTES

They have lots of flavors.

GUERRILLA 2

But say what they are. There's a sign out front.

FUENTES

There's chocolate, vanilla, mango – they have lots –

GUERRILLA 2

Say more – all of them –

FUENTES
(*sighs*)
Okay, chocolate, vanilla, mango, guava, coconut, guanabana, pineapple, strawberry, banana, coffee, orange – Let's see, hazelnut –

GUERRILLA 2

– they have rum flavor, don't they?

FUENTES

Rum, and tamarind – and something green. Like mint –

GUERRILLA 3

I want chocolate and coconut.

GUERRILLA 2

You only get to have one kind.

GUERRILLA 3

Why?

GUERRILLA 2

Because that's the rule.

GUERRILLA 3

How come you get to make the rule?

GUERRILLA 2
Because I've had ice-cream and you haven't.

FUENTES
Have you fought against the Army?

GUERRILLA 2
Sure. We're not just fucking around up here. We attack them
and they run and we get whatever guns and ammo they leave
behind.

GUERRILLA 3
But they never leave any food.

GUERRILLA 2
They know if they brought food we'd never leave them alone.

The Leader calls from under his blanket.

GUERRILLA I
Get to sleep, you two. We leave before sun-up. Sleep.

The boys settle down onto their blankets. Fuentes looks up at the stars.

GUERRILLA 3
Chocolate and mango.

EXT. JUNGLE – MORNING

*The strange family climbs through steep jungle. Fuentes fights to
breathe.*

EXT. CERCA DEL CIELO – MORNING

The Mother and the Young Girl cook tortillas on a comal *in front of a
meager hut. We can see now that the Mother's leg is lacerated and
badly discolored.*

YOUNG GIRL
What do you think they'll find?

MOTHER
It doesn't matter so much. When people start into a story
they have to see the end or they aren't happy.

YOUNG GIRL

How do the tortillas look?

MOTHER

They look like whoever made them doesn't know what she's doing.

She raises her head, seeming to hear something.

They're here.

She turns and we pan with her gaze to see Domingo, Fuentes, Graciela and Rabbit stumble out of the surrounding trees. They look wasted, especially the doctor. They give the Mother and her Daughter a dazed nod as they pass.

YOUNG GIRL

I'll ask him for you.

MOTHER

There's no hurry. He's come to stay.

EXT. CERCA DEL CIELO – DAY

We follow Fuentes and the others through the tiny settlement. It's not Paradise. Malnourished Indian People, shacks made of palm, a few chickens in wicker cages, a tiny field of corn that doesn't get enough sun. The Villagers watch us solemnly as we track through their encampment.

EXT. CERCA DEL CIELO – DAY

The visitors look around. An old Indian man, Viejo, approaches.

VIEJO

Welcome.

FUENTES

Hello.

VIEJO

You can stay here if you want. But here we live under the trees.

FUENTES

Where is the doctor?

97

VIEJO

There is no doctor here.

FUENTES

I heard she was with you. Dr Montoya.

Viejo shrugs.

VIEJO

This is where rumors go to die. Good luck.

He walks away. Fuentes sits heavily at the base of a huge tree.

DOMINGO

This village is fucked.

RABBIT

This is where the Sky People live. They eat air and shit clouds.

FUENTES

This is my legacy.

DOMINGO

Modelo looked better than this.

Fuentes is laughing bitterly.

FUENTES

Every man should leave a legacy – something he built, something he left in the world. Somebody he passed his knowledge to – one person to carry on for him. This is what I leave.

Fuentes smiles a peaceful smile.

At least I don't have to climb any more.

DOMINGO

The ruins looked better than this.

RABBIT

Is there anywhere else that would take you?

DOMINGO

There must be somewhere else. Somewhere even further on –

RABBIT

Can I have my two reales back?

DOMINGO

It's not what you had planned for your vacation, is it, Doctor?

Domingo turns to look at Fuentes. The doctor's eyes are closed. He doesn't breathe. Domingo goes to one knee to examine him.

Dead.

RABBIT

Really?

DOMINGO

He's dead.

Rabbit bends and stares at the doctor's face. Domingo stands, then picks up the black bag.

They'll steal this if we leave it here.

We hear the Young Girl off (don't translate).

Domingo turns to see the Young Girl standing there, looking fixedly at him, pointing to the bag. She says something in Indian and Rabbit answers (don't translate).

RABBIT
She says she needs a doctor.

DOMINGO
There is no doctor. The doctor is dead.

Rabbit translates. The Girl keeps pointing at the bag. She speaks again (don't translate).

RABBIT
She says there's a piece of metal in her mother's leg. She stepped on a mine the Army dropped from an airplane. She can't stand up.

DOMINGO
The doctor is dead.

The Girl keeps pointing at the bag. Domingo puts the bag down and takes a step away.

I'm not a doctor.

Graciela picks up the bag and holds it out to Domingo. He looks her in the eye for the first time, then looks to the Villagers. He sighs and turns to the Girl.

Okay. Where's your mother?

Domingo and Rabbit follow the Girl away. Graciela stays. She looks closely at Fuentes, then walks away through the trees.

Graciela steps into a clearing. She looks out at open sky and distant, jungle-covered mountaintops. She smiles.

LONE STAR

CREDITS

SAM DEEDS	Chris Cooper
PILAR CRUZ	Elizabeth Peña
DELMORE PAYNE	Joe Morton
OTIS PAYNE	Ron Canada
HOLLIS POGUE	Clifton James
CHARLEY WADE	Kris Kristofferson
BUDDY DEEDS	Matthew McConaughey
MERCEDES CRUZ	Miriam Colon
BUNNY	Frances McDormand
YOUNG HOLLIS	Jeff Monahan
YOUNG OTIS	Gabriel Casseus
YOUNG PILAR	Vanessa Martinez
YOUNG SAM	Tay Strathairn

Written, directed and edited by	John Sayles
Produced by	Maggie Renzi
	Paul Miller
Executive Producer	John Sloss
Director of Photography	Stuart Dryburgh
Production Design	Dan Bishop
Costume Design	Shay Cunliffe
Original Music	Mason Daring

A Sony Pictures Classics Release of a Castle Rock Entertainment
Presentation of a Rio Dulce Production.

EXT. TEXAS SCRUB – DAY

Two men in shorts and Hawaiian shirts are poking around a sandy section in the middle of scrub flats. Sergeant Cliff Potts is in the foreground, a plant and tree guidebook in hand, as Sergeant 'Mikey' Hogan works a metal detector over a large, sandy bank in the background. Both are Army career men with a morning off to pursue their hobbies.

> CLIFF

We got ocotillo, devil's walking stick – What's this stuff – It's that whattayoucallit – horse-crippler –

Mikey bends to scoop something out of the sand, putting it in a canvas bag slung on his hip.

> MIKEY

This place is a gold mine.

> CLIFF

Lead mine.

Mikey sees that Cliff is talking, pulls off his headset.

> MIKEY

What?

> CLIFF

It's a lead mine.

> MIKEY

Right.

> CLIFF

I don't know why I'm talking to you, you've got that thing on your head.

> MIKEY

You finding lots of cactus and shit?

                    CLIFF
It's not just cactus. There's the nopals, the yuccas –

                    MIKEY
              (*putting on headset*)
Looks like a lot of cactus to me.

                    CLIFF
                 (*grumbles*)
Man knows a hundred-fifty varieties of beer, he can't tell a
poinsettia from a prickly pear.

                    MIKEY
                 (*troubled*)
Cliff –

                    CLIFF
You live in a place, you should know something about it.
Explore –

                    MIKEY
Cliff –

CU: Mikey.

*Mikey in the foreground now, looking down at something as he pulls off
his headset again.*

      Cliff, you gotta look at this –

Cliff wearily turns and approaches from the background.

                    CLIFF
Don't tell me – Spanish treasure, right? Pieces of eight from
the Coronado expedition –

He stops by Mikey and looks down, his expression changing –

      Jesus –

*CU: bones. Sticking out from the sand bank are the skeletal bones of a
man's hand. There is a ring on one finger.*

                    MIKEY
                 (*off-screen*)
Was Coronado in the Masons?

LONE STAR

EXT. ROAD – DAY

A distant cloud of dust appears on the horizon.

Music underscores that we are in Texas, and we super-impose the opening credits as the dust takes form around an approaching car.

The car comes close enough to see it has a County Sheriff's insignia on the side.

INT. CAR – DAY

We see Sam Deeds, the Sheriff, driving. Sam is forty, quietly competent to the point of seeming a bit moody. He sees something up ahead. Music, credits end as Sam pulls off the road and we see Mikey and Cliff standing in the scrub.

EXT. SCRUB – DAY

The hand and forearm down to the elbow of the skeleton are visible now.

Wider: Cliff stands looking at the arm with Sam. Mikey is a few yards behind them, playing with his metal detector. Beyond him we see the Sheriff's car parked.

> SAM
>
> I was driving back from Apache Wells when they got me on the radio.

> CLIFF
>
> This was a rifle range way back when. But we figured it isn't Army land anymore, it's your jurisdiction –

> SAM
> (*nods*)
> I've got the forensics fella coming down from the Rangers. No way to know how old the body is without some lab work.

> CLIFF
>
> That ring –

> SAM
>
> Masons been around a long while.

Mikey has come up to them, still sweeping with the metal detector.

109

Treasure hunter?

> CLIFF
> (*apologetic*)
> Old bullets. He, uhm – makes art with them.

Sam just nods. Mikey frowns, goes down on one knee and scratches something out of the dirt at their feet.

> The Sheriff says we shouldn't touch anything, Mikey.
> (*to Sam*)
> He can't hear with that rig on – Mikey!

Mikey comes up with something, holds it before them. An encrusted piece of metal.

> MIKEY
> What've we got here?

Sam takes the thing, lays it back down where Mikey found it.

> SAM
> S'posed to leave everything right where we found it. They're
> real particular about that.

MIKEY

The scene of the crime.

SAM

No telling yet if there's been a crime.

Sam frowns down at the piece of metal as he rubs the face of it.

CU: metal.

Sam's thumb wipes across the face of the encrusted metal. It is roughly star-shaped.

(*off-screen*)

But this country's seen a good number of disagreements over the years.

INT. HIGH SCHOOL CLASSROOM – DAY

We look at a beautiful old pull-down map of Texas.

PILAR
(*off-screen*)

We do the best we can here –

A teacher in her late thirties, Pilar Cruz, steps in front of the map and we follow her across the room, carrying a poster.

– but, hey, public education these days is a bit of a battleground.

Posters hung on the walls beyond her show luminaries from Texas history: Sam Houston, Stephen Austin, Juan Seguin. A new parent, Celie Payne, stands in the middle of the otherwise empty classroom.

CELIE

He went to school on base when we were in Okinawa. It's all – you know – kids in the same boat – Army brats –

PILAR

His record shows that he's a good student.

CELIE

I'm more worried about the social thing. Are there like – gangs, or –?

Pilar starts to put the poster up. Celie moves to hold it in place for her –

PILAR

We haven't had any serious violence, if that's what you mean. We've got a pretty lively mix though – You walk into the cafeteria and the Anglo kids are in one section, the Mexican kids in another and the black kids have a table in the back – thanks –

CELIE

So blacks are –

PILAR

They're the smallest group except for a couple Kickapoo kids. Look, you're obviously a concerned parent. Chet has no history of getting into trouble – I'm happy to have him in my class.

She steps back to see if the poster, an old photo of Geronimo, is straight. Another teacher, Molly, sticks her head in the door.

> MOLLY
> (*uncomfortable*)
> Pilar? Is uhm – is Amado okay?

> PILAR
> Okay? He's not here?

> MOLLY
> No. Is he sick?

> PILAR
> (*mutters*)
> He's going to wish he was dead.

EXT. STREET – DAY

CU: vaquero picture.

On the door of a deluxe pickup truck is an airbrushed picture of a Pancho Villa-looking vaquero with bandoliers crossing his chest and a gun blazing in each hand. We hear loud music.

> AMADO
> (*off-screen*)
> Luis! Give me that Phillips-head back –

Wider: a small group of teenage Chicano Boys hang around the truck in the bed, on the hood, leaning against it. A boom-box placed on top of the cab blasts banda music out at the neighborhood. Somebody's legs are hanging out the open passenger-side door. The Kids suddenly look as a Sheriff's Department car slides into the foreground. A deputy sheriff, Travis, gets out.

Kids try to look tough and unworried as we track across the street toward them. Travis's hand reaches out from behind the camera to flick off the music.

INT. PICKUP – DAY

Amado Cruz, Pilar's fifteen-year-old son, lies on the front seat installing a compact disc player into the dash slot. He reaches up to the dash, can't find what he wants.

AMADO
Somebody hand me the CD player – *dámelo, pendejos* –

He looks up and we tilt to see Travis leaning in the window, examining the new radio.

TRAVIS
They come a long way from those old eight-track jobs, haven't they?

AMADO
Something wrong?

TRAVIS
(*waves radio*)
This is stolen property. Alla you fellas are coming down to the station.

INT. CAFÉ SANTA BARBARA – AFTERNOON

Sweat beads the forehead of a thin, tired-looking recent immigrant, Enrique, as he delivers platters of chile rellenos to a booth. Mexican music plays on a jukebox in the background. We hold on the booth, where Hollis Pogue, in his sixties, entertains two good old boys.

HOLLIS
So Buddy walks up to the porch and there's old Fishbait McHenry, cleanin' the dirt out his toenails with a pocket-knife – He was the most hygienic of all the McHenrys –

The breakfast companions are laughing already.

'Fishbait,' says Buddy, in that quiet way of his, 'what you know about them tires that went missing from Merkel's?' Fishbait thinks for a minute, then he lifts up a loose board from the porch floor and calls down into it, 'C'mon out, Pooter, they caught us!'

FENTON
(*laughing*)
Buddy Deeds. He had a way.

HOLLIS
He known who it was onnaconna the tire tracks in the dirt from the back of the garage to where they loaded up. 'Old Fishbait,' he says, 'never lifted a thing in this world if there was a way he could *roll* it.'

More laughter.

FENTON
Won't be another like him. That boy of his doesn't come near it. You ask me, he's all hat and no cattle.

SAM
(*off-screen*)
Fellas –

We widen to see Sam standing by their booth. No telling how long he's been listening. Fenton is embarrassed.

HOLLIS
Sam! I was just telling a few about your old man.

FENTON
He was a unique individual.

SAM

Yeah, he was that.

We sense a little strain when Sam has to talk about his father.

HOLLIS

Big day coming up – I wish we'd have thought of it while he was still living. But he went so unexpected –

FENTON

Better late than never. Korean War hero, Sheriff for near thirty years – Buddy Deeds Memorial P –

SAM

I heard there was a bit of a fuss.

HOLLIS

Oh, you know, the usual troublemakers. Danny Padilla from the *Sentinel*, that crowd –

FENTON

Every other damn thing in the country is called after Martin Luther King, they can't let our side have one measly park?

HOLLIS

King wasn't Mexican, Fenton –

FENTON

Bad enough all the street names are in Spanish –

SAM

They were here first –

FENTON

Then name it after Big Chief Shitinabucket! Whoever that Tonkawa fella was. He had the Mexes beat by centuries –

HOLLIS

There was a faction pulling for that boy who was killed in the Gulf War – Ruben –

SAM

– Santiago.

HOLLIS

Right. But nobody here ever noticed him till they read his name on the national news –

FENTON

They just wanted it to be one of theirs –

HOLLIS

That's not the whole story. The Mexicans that *know*, that *remember*, understand what Buddy was for their people. Hell, it was Mercedes over there who swung the deciding vote for him.

Sam looks to the register where Pilar's mother, Mercedes Cruz, whacks rolls of change apart on the counter. She seems to be avoiding looking toward him.

SAM

That so?

HOLLIS

She put it even at three to three, so as the Mayor I get to cast the tie-breaker. The older generation won't have any problem with it. They remember how Buddy come to be Sheriff, that it was all 'cause he took their part.

FENTON

Tell that one, Hollis –

HOLLIS

Hell, everybody heard that story a million times –

SAM

I'd like to hear it. Your version of it.

Something about the way Sam says it puts Hollis on guard.

FENTON

Go ahead, Hollis.

CU: Hollis. He's hooked into it now.

HOLLIS

The two of us were the only deputies back then – me and Buddy – it's what – '58 –

FENTON
(*off-screen*)

'57, I believe –

HOLLIS

And the Sheriff at the time was Big Charley Wade. Charley was one of your old-fashioned bribe-or-bullets kind of sheriffs, he took a healthy bite out of whatever moved through this county –

He looks down at the table.

It was in here one night, back when Jimmy Herrera run the place. Started right here in this booth –

We pan down to the table. The food has changed. The tortillas are in a straw basket instead of plastic. The jukebox changes to another song and the light dims slightly. A hand with a big Masonic ring on one finger appears to lift a tortilla – underneath it lie three ten-dollar bills. The hand lifts them up and we tilt to see the face of Sheriff Charley Wade, a big, mean redneck with shrewd eyes.

It is 1957.

WADE
(*grins*)

This beaner fare doesn't agree with me, but the price sure is right.

Wider: Wade sits across from his young deputies, Young Hollis (thirties) and Buddy Deeds (twenties). A chicken-fried steak sits untouched in front of Buddy. Hollis has the anxious look of an errand boy, while Buddy is self-contained and quietly forceful for his age.

BUDDY

What's that for?

WADE

Jimmy got a kitchen full of wetbacks, most of 'em relatives. People breed like chickens.

BUDDY

So?

WADE

I roust some *muchacho* on the street, doesn't have his papers, all he got to say is '*Yo trabajo para Jimmy Herrera.*'

Wade folds the money and stuffs it in his pocket.

You got to keep the wheels greased, son. Sheriff does his job right, everybody makes out. Now this is gonna be one of your pickups, Buddy. First of the month, just like the rent. Get the car, Hollis.

Wade and Hollis slide out of the booth to stand.

BUDDY

I'm not doing it.

Hollis stops a few feet away, shocked. Wade just stares down at Buddy.

WADE

Come again?

Buddy looks Wade in the eye, seemingly unafraid.

BUDDY

It's your deal. You sweated it out of him, *you* pick it up.

> WADE

There's gonna be some left over for you, Buddy. I take care of my boys.

> BUDDY

That's not the point.

> WADE

You feeling bad for Jimmy? Have him tell you the size of the *mordida* they took out of his hide when he run a place on the other side. Those old boys in Ciudad León.

> BUDDY

I'm not picking it up.

> WADE

You do whatever I say you do or else you put it on the *trail*, son.

The Customers are all watching now, nervous. Buddy thinks for a moment, not taking his eyes off Wade.

> BUDDY

How 'bout this – how 'bout you put that shield on this table and vanish before you end up dead or in jail?

Wade rests his hand on his pistol. It is dead silent but for the music on the box.

You ever shoot anybody was looking you in the eye?

> WADE

Who said anything about shootin' anybody?

Buddy has his gun out under the table. He slowly brings it up and lays it flat on the table, not taking his hand off it or his eyes off Wade.

> BUDDY

Whole different story, isn't it?

> WADE

You're fired. You're outta the department.

> BUDDY

There's not a soul in this county isn't sick to death of your

121

bullshit, Charley. You made yourself scarce, you could make a lot of people happy.

WADE

You little pissant –

BUDDY

Now or later, Charley. You won't have any trouble finding me.

Wade feels the people around him waiting for a reaction. He leans close to Buddy to croak in a hoarse whisper.

WADE

You're a dead man.

He turns and nearly bumps into Hollis. He gives the Deputy a shove.

Get the goddam car. We're going to Roderick's.

CU: Buddy. He watches till the screen door shuts behind them, then holsters his gun and begins to saw at the steak as if nothing had happened. He calls softly.

BUDDY

Muchacho – más cerveza por favor.

He looks up at somebody and we pan till we see Sam, still standing over the booth, listening.

We are back in 1995.

> HOLLIS
> (*off-screen*)
'*Más cerveza por favor.*'

> FENTON
> (*off-screen*)
That Buddy was a cool breeze.

We pull back to see Hollis and his buddies at the table, eating their lunches as they listen.

Charley Wade were known to have put a good number of people in the *ground*, and your daddy gets eyeball to eyeball with him.

> HOLLIS
We made our collection at Roderick's place and that was the last anybody seen hide nor hair of him. He went missing the next day, along with ten thousand dollars in county funds from the safe at the jail.

> SAM
Never heard from him again?

> HOLLIS
Not a peep. Buddy run the man out of town.

> FENTON
Buddy Deeds said a thing, he damn well backed it up. Won't be another like him.

> SAM
So he arrested all of Jimmy Herrara's people and sent 'em back to the other side?

Hollis sees what Sam is getting at, grins.

> HOLLIS
Oh – he come to an accommodation. Money doesn't always need to change hands to keep the wheels turning.

        SAM

Right.

        HOLLIS

Look, I know you had some problems with your father, and
he and Muriel – well –

        FENTON

Your mother was a saint.

        HOLLIS

– but Buddy Deeds was my sal*va*tion.

Sam nods, speaks softly.

        SAM

Won't be another like him.

EXT. ARMY INSTALLATION – DAY

CU: Del Payne.

*Colonel Delmore Payne (Del), a very direct, by-the-book black officer,
addresses a group of officers and NCOs. Artillery piece angle toward the
sky behind him.*

DEL

– it's an honor for me to assume command of this unit, and I look forward to working with all of you.

Cliff and Mikey, in uniform now, flank Sergeant Priscilla Worth, a black woman in her early forties, as they stand in formation.

(*off-screen*)
I'm sure you're all aware of the Army's decision to close this installation under the Reduction in Force plan. That does not mean, however –

Reverse. We look over the shoulders of assembled Officers and NCOs toward Del.

– that we've been sent here to mark time until we are absorbed by another unit.

CU: Del.

You may have heard rumors that I run a very tight operation. These rumors are not exaggerated.

INT. SHERIFF'S OFFICE – AFTERNOON

We are looking through a magnifying glass at an old photo. Buddy's face is slightly distorted by the glass.

SECRETARY
(*off-screen*)
Sam? I got Danny Padilla from the paper for you –

Sam sits at his desk in the Sheriff's office, looking down at the photo.

SAM
Tell him I'll catch him later.

CU: photograph. An old photo of the 1957 Sheriff's Department officers on the courthouse steps. Wade, Hollis, Buddy, a few others, all in uniform.

SECRETARY
(*off-screen*)
He says he needs to talk to you before the ceremony.

Sam puts a magnifying glass over the photo and bends close to look.

SAM

Tell him to try me tomorrow.

Extreme CU: photo. A magnified POV of the badge on Wade's chest swims into view. A metal star. We hear the Secretary getting rid of the caller.

SECRETARY
(*off-screen*)

He thinks you're trying to duck him.

CU: Sam looking at the photo, troubled.

SAM
(*mutters*)

He's right.

EXT. BIG O'S ROADHOUSE – NIGHT

We start on a blinking neon sign – BIG O'S, then pan to see a full parking lot outside the low, neon-lit roadhouse. R & B music blasts from inside.

EXT. DOORWAY – NIGHT

Chet, a black kid around fifteen, stands nervously at the door building up his courage. He takes a deep breath, plunges in.

INT. BIG O'S – NIGHT

We track with Chet, very nervous, as he makes his way through the crowded roadhouse. The customers are all black, many from the nearby Army post, shouting and laughing over the loud music. Chet, edgy, is looking for somebody. He sees:

Chet's POV: Otis. Seen through the crush is Otis 'Big O' Payne, a large man in his early sixties, laughing as he stands behind the bar.

Chet nervously puts his hand under his jacket. A gun? He pushes forward to get a better view.

Chet's POV: Moving in on Otis. Otis looks over, sees the boy, frowns.

Chet reaches under his jacket. He pulls out a photograph. He looks at it – suddenly there is a scream from behind, then gunshots, patrons diving for the floor. Chet whirls around and we whip pan to see a young man, Shadow, emptying his pistol into Richie, a young soldier, as a young woman, Athena, screams and tries to pull the gun away. With the last shot, Shadow turns and heads for the door, but is tackled and swarmed by angry Men, shouting. We pan to Athena, kneeling over the bleeding, twitching body of Richie.

Chet backs up, horrified. A large hand grasps him on the shoulder from behind. He turns to see Otis standing over him, strangely calm amid the chaos.

OTIS

You weren't in here tonight, were you?

CHET

No sir.

OTIS
(points)

Go out through the back.

Chet hurries away. Otis watches him for a moment, then turns to the mess in his club.

INT. AUDITORIUM – NIGHT

CU: Anglo Mother, an angry woman, standing from her auditorium chair.

> ANGLO MOTHER
>
> You're just tearin' everything down! Tearin' down our heritage, tearin' down our history, tearin' down the memory of people that fought and died for this land –

> CHICANO FATHER
> (*off-screen*)
>
> We fought and died for this land, too!

We whip pan to see another standing parent.

> We fought the US Army, the Texas Rangers –

> ANGLO FATHER
> (*off-screen*)
>
> Yeah, but you *lost*, buddy!

We whip pan to a man in the rear.

> Winners get the bragging rights, that's how it goes –

> PRINCIPAL
> (*off-screen*)
>
> People – people –

Wider: we are in the high school auditorium, a hot-and-heavy teachers and parents meeting in progress. Pilar sits at the end of a long table facing the agitated parents, taking some heat. Danny Padilla, a young, long-haired reporter, sits in the front taking notes, enjoying the show.

> I think it would be best not to put things in terms of winners and losers –

> ANGLO MOTHER
> (*points at Pilar*)
>
> Well, the way she's teachin' it has got everything switched

around. I was on the textbook committee, and her version is
not –

PRINCIPAL

We think of the textbook as kind of a guide, not an absolute.

ANGLO MOTHER

– it is not what we set as the *stan*dard! Now you people can
believe what you want, but when it comes to teaching our
children –

CHICANO MOTHER

They're our children, too!

ANGLO FATHER

The men who founded this state have a right to have their
story –

DANNY

The men who founded this state broke from Mexico because
they needed slavery to be legal to make a fortune in the cotton
business!

PILAR

I think that's a bit of an oversimplification –

ANGLO FATHER

Are you reporting this meeting or runnin' it, Danny?

DANNY

Just adding a little historical perspective –

*Rear of auditorium: Paloma Cruz, Pilar's teenage daughter, peeks into
the room, then moves down the side toward the stage.*

ANGLO FATHER

You may call it history, but I call it propaganda. I'm sure they
got their own account of the Alamo on the other side, but
we're not *on* the other side, so we're not about to have it
taught in our schools!

PILAR

There's no reason to be so threatened by this –

Pilar is trying to stay calm despite her anger.

I've only been trying to get across some of the complexity of our situation down here – cultures coming together in both negative and positive ways –

ANGLO MOTHER
(*off-screen*)
If you mean like music and food and all, I have no problem with that –

We shoot past Pilar toward the Parents in their seats. Paloma steps up to whisper to her.

– but when you start changing who did what to who –

TEACHER
We're not *chan*ging anything, we're presenting a more complete picture –

ANGLO MOTHER
And that's what's got to stop!

Pilar looks troubled by what she's heard. She shoots a look toward the others at the table, then slips away with Paloma.

TEACHER
There's enough ignorance in the world without us encouraging it in the classroom –

ANGLO MOTHER
Now who are you calling ignorant?

PRINCIPAL
Folks, I know this is a very emotional issue for some of you, but we have other business to attend to –

CHICANO FATHER
We're not going to get some resolution on this?

CU: Principal – weary.

PRINCIPAL
Would you people like to form another committee?

Groans from the Parents.

INT. SHERIFF'S OFFICE – NIGHT

Shadow, face bruised, hands cuffed behind him, is pushed in through the door to be booked.

> SHADOW
>
> I hope the sucker does die, man! Mess with me, that's what you get!

Sam steps in behind him and meets his chief deputy, Ray Hernandez, coming from the other direction.

> RAY
>
> Hospital says the other kid is in bad shape –

> SAM
> *(glances ahead)*
>
> The shooter local?

> RAY
> *(shakes his head)*
>
> Down from Houston. I think he knew the girl before.

> SAM
>
> Okay – we'll take a statement from all the GIs before they go back to post. You can get the story from Otis over at the club.

> RAY
>
> Any poop on the John Doe you found out there today?

> SAM
>
> Nothin' much. The Rangers put Ben Wetzel on it. Catch you later.

As Ray steps out, Pilar, looking distraught, walks into the station, passing right by Sam without seeing him.

CU: Sam. He wonders what she's doing there.

Sam's POV: Pilar. She stands by an unoccupied reception desk, very upset, unable to attract anyone's attention because of the activity around the shooting. She looks tired and a bit scared under the harsh overhead light.

(*off-screen*)

Pilar?

Pilar looks around. Sam is standing by her. We can tell there is some history between these two.

Something wrong?

PILAR

They've got my Amado.

SAM

Got him here?

PILAR

Somebody called – something about an electronics store –

SAM

I'll see what's going on.

He starts away, stops, comes back.

I was – I was real sorry about Nando. He was a good fella. We haven't talked since –

PILAR

We haven't talked since high school.

SAM

Yeah. I'll go check on your boy.

Pilar watches Sam go.

As the rear of the office Travis sits typing away at a word processor as Athena, in tears, gives testimony.

ATHENA

– so Richie just didn't say nothin' 'cause he didn't want to get into it, see, and the next thing I know there's shots and Richie is down. It happened so *fast* –

SAM

(*off-screen*)

Excuse me –

We widen to see Sam standing over the desk.

We got some boys you run in earlier today?

TRAVIS

Yeah. I pulled the bunch that hangs at Pico Bernal's place.
We finally caught them with something.

SAM

You got a juvenile with 'em – Amado Cruz?

Travis looks at his booking sheets.

TRAVIS

Yeah – let's see – the other ones say he wasn't in on the theft,
he just knows how to hook things up. We've been trying to
contact a parent –

INT. JAIL HALLWAY – NIGHT

Sam walks with Amado, who is trying to look defiant.

SAM

They tell me you're good at fixing things.

Nothing.

Your father was a hell of a mechanic.

Still nothing.

You know, if you figure minimum wage on the time most
thieves spend in jail, they could have bought most everything
they stole.

AMADO

I didn't steal anything.

SAM

I didn't say you did. My name is Sam, by the way.

Amado just gives him a look.

INT. SHERIFF'S OFFICE – NIGHT

Sam and Amado step out into the office, where Pilar stands waiting.

SAM

He's all yours.

PILAR

Are you okay?

AMADO

I don't know what the big deal is.

PILAR

You'll find out when I get you home. Thanks, Sam.

SAM

No problem.

Pilar yanks Amado outside by his arm. She turns to shoot a look back at Sam, then steps out through the glass door.

CU: Sam watching her go.

Any time.

FADE OUT

EXT. OBSTACLE COURSE – MORNING

We shoot up from a pit in the ground. Whump! Whump! Whump! Three men leap over, landing on the far side and running away from us.

Del Payne runs with Cliff and Mikey on a pathway along a security fence, the two sergeants struggling to keep up, occasionally vaulting or scaling some mild obstacle.

MIKEY

There's not that much down here, Colonel. Big O's is the only place in the county that our African American soldiers are, uhm – that they feel comfortable in.

DEL

Have we had trouble there before?

CLIFF

Since I've been stationed here? A fist fight now and then.

MIKEY

We had a kid pass out in the men's room. The town isn't
much –

DEL

They didn't come for a vacation.

CLIFF

Yes, sir.

MIKEY

You know how it is, Colonel – first time away from home,
dealing with new people – I remember my first hitch –

DEL

Substance abuse?

MIKEY

Well, yeah, but I went through the Program. I haven't had a
drink since –

DEL

I meant on the post. In general. How are you dealing with it?

CLIFF

We throw a urine test at them once a month. Random
numbers, maybe a hundred people at a time –

DEL

Why don't we make it once a week for a while?

CLIFF

No problem, sir.

Del notices how hard they are breathing.

DEL

I sprint the last quarter-mile. You gentlemen don't have to
keep up if you don't care to.

MIKEY

Appreciate it, sir.

Del accelerates and we hold with the sergeants, slowing to a near walk.

MIKEY

Guy cracks walnuts with his asshole.

CLIFF
(grins)
You get the feeling he doesn't want to be here?

INT. FORENSICS LAB – DAY

We heard Hank Williams's gospel song 'I'll Have a New Body (I'll Have a New Life)' as we see the gathered bones of the skeleton tagged and photographed and measured, impressions made of the dental work in the skull, photographs of the excavation of the body at various stages marked with red grease pencil, the piece of metal laid in a detarnishing dish, the ring put under a microscope.

CU: metal.

Music continues as we tighten on the piece of metal, a pair of tongs pulling it from the detarnishing solution. It is a star-shaped badge, bearing the words 'SHERIFF – RIO COUNTY '.

INT. COUNTRY AND WESTERN BAR – AFTERNOON

C & W music playing, the regulars starting to show up. Sam makes his way to a table where Ben Wetzel, a Texas Ranger, sits with a file of forensic reports.

BEN

Sam the Man.

SAM

Hey, Ben. Thanks for coming down.

They shake, Sam sits.

BEN

How's business.

SAM

Business is booming. Got your drugs, got your illegals – had shooting the other night at Big O's. Soldier got ventilated.

BEN

I hear they're closing that post down.

SAM

September '97, that's all she wrote.

BEN

Gonna pull a lot of jobs out of this county.

SAM

Yeah, we'll have folks swimming over to Mexico to work in the sweatshops.

Sam looks at the folder of reports.

That the word on our boy?

BEN

Yeah, this is Skinny.

SAM

Skinny?

BEN

We find a body, it's either Skinny or Stinky, depending on how much meat there is on the bones.

SAM

Nice job.

BEN
(*opens folder*)

Male, forty to fifty years old, five-foot-eleven, chewed tobacco – then we get into the dental records –

SAM

Charley Wade.

BEN
(*nods*)

That badge –

SAM

It didn't come out of a cereal box.

137

BEN

Yeah.

SAM

You know the popular version of how he left town –

BEN

Everybody on the border knows that story.

SAM

You got a cause of death?

BEN

Skull was intact, no soft tissue left – not much to go on.

SAM

So he could have gone out to the base, hopped the fence, dug down into the dirt on the old rifle range and had a heart attack.

Ben smiles, closes the folder.

BEN

You, uhm – you remember what old Buddy carried for a side arm?

SAM

Colt Peacemaker.

BEN

A .45 –

SAM

He swore by it.

Ben frowns.

What?

BEN

Just wondering –

SAM

So is Buddy on your short list?

BEN

If it was some poor *mojado*, swam across at night, got lost in

138

the scrub and starved out there, we wouldn't go any further.
But this is a formerly prominent citizen –

SAM

You got to investigate. No question about it.

BEN

What I will do is keep names out of it till we got some
answers or hit a dead end. You know how the press is with a
murder story – even if it's forty years old.

SAM

Yeah, it's a pretty cold trail.

They sit in awkward silence for a moment. Ben feels bad about this.

BEN

I remember Charley Wade come to my father's hardware
store once when I was a little boy. I'd heard stories how he
shot this one, how he shot that one – man winked at me and I
peed in my pants.
                    (*shaking his head*)
Winked at me.

INT. CLASSROOM – DAY

*Pilar stands at the blackboard by her outline of nineteenth-century
Texas history.*

PILAR

Okay, we have the fight against the Spanish with bloody
conflict for dozens of years till they're finally defeated in 1821
and Mexican independence is declared. Anglo settlers are
invited.

*CU: drawing. Somebody making a skillful pencil drawing on the corner
of a sheet of lined notebook paper. A bald, muscular shot-putter after
releasing the shot, his hand large in the foreground.*

(*off-screen*)

– to colonize the area and by the time they begin the
movement against Santa Anna they outnumber the Mexicans
here by four to one. The war between Mexico –

139

Chet is drawing intently. He takes the notebook and lays his thumb over the corner.

> – and the Anglo forces ends in 1836 with the formation of the Texas Republic. Texas joins the United States as a state where slavery is legal in 1845 –

Notebook: Chet 'flips' the corner of the notebook and the series of drawings he's made form a brief cartoon of the shot-putter blowing his cheeks out and heaving the shot right past us. Extremely well drawn.

> – after the so-called Mexican war and then secedes to join the Confederacy in 1861. The Confederacy is beaten, and the Reformation period here is marked by range wars and race wars –

Pilar looks out at the class.

> – and all this paralleled by constant battles between both the Mexican and Anglo settlers and the various Indian nations in the area. What are we seeing here? Chet?

Chet, startled, hides the notebook under his hands.

CHET

Uhm – everybody is killing everybody else?

EXT. LAKE – DAY

CU: fishing lure. A nasty-looking thing. Only a bass would want to eat this. Hollis leans in to peer at the thing dangling before his face.

Wider: Hollis sits in the swivel chair of a bass boat tied to a dock at the lake, going through his box of lures. Sam appears on the dock and steps down.

SAM

I always wondered what you Mayors do when you're not cutting ribbons –

HOLLIS

Sam! Hey podner! You caught me playing hooky –

SAM
(*looking across lake*)
Floating around out here, playin' hell with them bass – play a little cards, play a little golf, drink some beer –

HOLLIS
Sounds great. Where do I sign up?

SAM
I haven't been out here for a while.

HOLLIS
You go by your old house?

SAM
No.

HOLLIS
Just as well. The new people just painted it some God-awful color –

SAM
We found a body out by the Army post yesterday. Been there for a long time.

Hollis squints at a rubbery lure, rejects it.

HOLLIS
Was it Davy Crockett or Jim Bowie?

SAM
(*smiles*)
You recall if Charley Wade was a Mason?

HOLLIS
Charley? I believe he was. Used to go for lodge meetings over to Laredo. What's he got to do with your body?

SAM
All it was wearing was a big old Masonic ring and a Rio County Sheriff's badge.

Hollis reacts. Sam puts a foot on the gunwale of the boat.

You don't remember anything else from that last night you saw him, do you?

HOLLIS

I told the story enough times – hell, we were just in the car,
he was stewing about the fight with Buddy while we drove
over to Roderick Bledsoe's –

SAM

Bledsoe?

HOLLIS

He owned the colored roadhouse before Big O –

SAM

He still living?

HOLLIS

No. I think his widow's still in their place in Darktown,
though.
                    (*shaking his head*)
You think it's Charley Wade, huh?

SAM

Forensics people are sure of it. You have any idea who might
have put him there?

Hollis makes a great show of considering.

Besides my father, I mean.

HOLLIS

There's no call for that, Sam. Fella made himself a pile of
enemies over the years.

SAM

And Buddy was one of them.

HOLLIS

We got that dedication tomorrow. This is a hell of a time to
be draggin' up old business –

SAM

People have worked this whole big thing up around my father.
If it's built on a crime, they deserve to know. Now I
understand why you might want to believe he couldn't do it –

HOLLIS

And I understand why you might want to think he *could*.

This is a low blow, but accurate enough to shake Sam up.

SAM

Thanks for your time, Hollis.

Hollis holds up a double handful of lures – dozens of rubber and plastic worms and shiners and frogs and spinners.

HOLLIS

Look at all this, would you? My tackle, the boat – all to catch a little old fish just minding its business on the bottom of the lake.

He gives Sam a look.

Hardly seems worth the effort – does it, Sam?

Sam walks away.

INT. CLASSROOM – ARMY BASE – DAY

CU: Athena. She stands at attention, trying to keep her composure.

CLIFF
(*off-screen*)
So you knew this young man before?

ATHENA

From back in Houston. We both come up on Fifth Street.

PRISCILLA
(*off-screen*)
Did you know he was going to be there last night?

ATHENA

If I had I wouldn't have gone in.

PRISCILLA
(*off-screen*)
And you and Private Graves –

ATHENA

We were just dancing –

Wider: Cliff leans against a desk, a blackboard covered with radar diagrams behind him. Priscilla sits nearby, both of them focused on Athena.

> PRISCILLA
> We're not running a dating service here.

> ATHENA
> I know that, Sergeant. We were just dancing. There was a bunch of us there. Shadow just come down looking for trouble.

> CLIFF
> It's not our job to get involved in your personal life, but when it interferes with the training here –

> ATHENA
> I'm sorry, Sergeant Major. There wasn't anything I could do. Shadow gets crazy.

A silence as the sergeants let her stew for a moment. She works up her courage.

> Sergeant Major? How is Richie doing? Private Graves?

> CLIFF
> He'll live.

> PRISCILLA
> He'll be transferred to a military hospital as soon as he's stabilized –

> CLIFF
> He'll probably be getting a medical discharge –

> ATHENA
> Out of the Army?

> CLIFF
> He's going to lose a lung.

This is not good news for Athena.

> ATHENA
> Will this go on my record?

Cliff considers for a long moment.

> CLIFF
>
> If the incident happened the way you say it did, there hasn't been an infraction.

> ATHENA
>
> Thank you, Sergeant Major.

> CLIFF
>
> You're dismissed.

> ATHENA
>
> Thank you, Sergeant Major.

Athena steps out of the room. Cliff sits on the desk.

> PRISCILLA
>
> You spoil 'em, Cliff.

> CLIFF
>
> Hey – she's in a tough situation. I cut her some slack –

> PRISCILLA
>
> But I'm the one in charge of her sorry ass.

> CLIFF
> (*crossing to the door*)
> She's pulled herself out of a pretty rough neighborhood –

> PRISCILLA
>
> And if she isn't careful she's gonna slide right back into it.

EXT. BLEDSOE HOUSE – DAY

We start on a CU of a rocker creaking back and forth on an old wooden porch. A woman hums.

Minnie Bledsoe, in her sixties, sits on her porch in the old black section of town, playing with a Gameboy. She has on very thick glasses. Sam walks up to her from his car.

> SAM
>
> Mrs Bledsoe?

MINNIE

That's me.

SAM

I'm Sheriff Deeds –

MINNIE

Sheriff Deeds's dead, honey – you just Sheriff Junior.

SAM
(*smiles*)
Yeah, that's the story of my life.

MINNIE

You ever play one of these?

SAM

I've seen 'em.

MINNIE

Well, don't ever start up on 'em, 'cause once you do you can't stop. I tell myself I'm gonna play just three little games after breakfast, and here I sit with half the day gone.

SAM

You mind if I ask a few questions about your husband? Roderick?

MINNIE

I won't say nothing bad about the man, but you can ask away.

SAM

He had the club out on the old trail road –

MINNIE

We run that twenty-odd years. Give it over to Otis Payne in 1967. April.

SAM

So you must remember Sheriff Wade.

MINNIE

Not if I can help it.

SAM

You had to deal with him in running the club.

MINNIE

Them days, you deal with Sheriff Wade or you didn't deal at all. First of the month, every month, he remind you of who you really workin' for.

SAM

He squeezed money out of you?

MINNIE

Wasn't legal to sell liquor in a glass back then unless you was a *club*, see. Roderick used to say, 'Buy yourself a drink, you get a free membership.' But Sheriff Wade, he could shut you down anytime.

SAM

And my father?

MINNIE

Sheriff Buddy was a different story. Long as Roderick throw his weight the right way on election day, make sure all the colored get out to vote – we was called colored back then, if you was polite – maybe throw a barbecue for the right people now and then, things was peaceful. That Sheriff Wade, though, he took an awful big bite.

SAM

People didn't complain?

MINNIE

Not if they was colored or Meskin. Not if they wanted to keep breathin'.

SAM

Do you remember the last time you saw him?

Minie thinks, puts down the Gameboy.

MINNIE

I seen him in our place the last week before he gone missin'.

We track in to a CU of her. R & B music fades up slowly.

147

He used to come in whilst we was in full swing, make people nervous. Had him a smile like the Grim Reaper –

DISSOLVE TO:

INT. ROADHOUSE – 1957 – NIGHT

The joint is crowded, people drinking, talking, laughing, a few dancing, all trying to avoid locking eyes with Sheriff Wade, who sits with his legs stretched out at a table. Young Hollis sits by him, smiling uncomfortably. Sax-wailing R & B blasts from the jukebox. Young Otis, a slick, confident character with straightened hair and a silk shirt on, in his early twenties, stops to talk with a Man on his way to bring a tray with a couple beers and glasses over.

> MINNIE
> (*voice-over*)
> – just sit back with his hand on that big ol' gun and act the kingfish with everybody. Otis Payne had come to work for us by then, and that boy had him some *atti*tude –

CU: Wade watching Young Otis with narrowed eyes.

CU: Wade's POV – Otis.

A Man puts a slip of paper in Otis's pocket, pats his back. Otis winks to acknowledge the bet, turns, makes eyes at a Pretty Woman sitting at the bar, who is eyeing him back. He lays the beers and glasses on the table, starts away.

> WADE

Pour it.

Otis turns, cups his hand around his ear.

Pour it.

Expressionless, he starts to pour the beer into Wade's glass. The Sheriff looks up into his face.

I know you?

> YOUNG OTIS

Name's Otis.

WADE

Otis what?

YOUNG OTIS

Payne.

WADE

One of Cleroe Payne's boys?

YOUNG OTIS

Uh-huh.

WADE

I sent your Daddy to the farm once.

YOUNG OTIS

I know that.

WADE

Why you think that was?

Otis feels people watching. He doesn't want to lose face.

YOUNG OTIS

Some crop needed pickin' and the man was shorthanded.

A very insolent answer for the time and place.

WADE

As I remember it was because he had a sassy mouth on him.
Must run in the family. You wouldn't be runnin' numbers
out of this club, now, would you, son?

YOUNG OTIS

Runnin' numbers illegal.

WADE

Runnin' numbers without I know about it is both illegal and
un*healthy*. You remember that.

The beer is poured. Otis starts away.

Whoah, son. You're not finished. Pour his.

YOUNG HOLLIS

I prefer it in the bottle –

WADE

Shut up, Hollis. Pour.

Otis meets Wade's look now, pours the other beer.

How come you don't look familiar?

YOUNG OTIS

Been away. Up to Houston.

WADE

Houston, huh? I hear they let you boys run wild up there.

No response. Wade deliberately pushes the glass away so beer splashes on the table and drips into Hollis's lap.

Aw – look what you done now. Better get something to wipe it up, son.

Half the people in the room are watching now, the other half moving away to relative safety. Otis tries to keep a lid on his temper, looks around the room.

YOUNG OTIS

You spilt it, you wipe it up.

Wade stands, steely-eyed, and looks at Otis nose to nose.

WADE

I told you to do something. Are you gonna hop to it, or are we gonna have a problem?

Otis is starting to shake, but holds his ground.

Don't want to turn tail in front of your people. I understand.

He starts to turn away then whap! *brings the butt of his pistol up under Otis's chin, knocking him to the floor. A Woman screams and Otis, enraged, grabs the chair he has fallen over, starts to get up – but Wade has the pistol levelled at his face.*

Come on, Houston, give it a try! Come to Poppa –

Roderick is out on the floor now, hands held out in a gesture of peace, as Young Minnie watches from behind the bar, petrified.

RODERICK

Don't mind him, Sheriff. Boy's just a bit slow, is all. He don't
mean nothin' by it –

WADE

That the problem, son? You slow?

RODERICK

Otis, apologize to the Sheriff –

Otis eases the chair down but doesn't say anything.

You got him too scared to peep, Sheriff. Maybe if you put
that gun up –

WADE

You telling me what to do, Roderick?

RODERICK

No, Sheriff, I'm just –

Wade looks around, widens his eyes in mock surprise.

WADE

What's this I see? Is that whiskey in them glasses on the bar?
Roderick, I'm onna have to cite you for a violation of State
law –

RODERICK

This is a club, Sheriff – you been in here –

WADE

All you people better clear out of here! Now!

A few people start for the exit. Wade swivels and blam! *sends a bullet
past Minnie that shatters a crystal decanter behind the bar. People run
for the door. Wade squats down to look Otis in the face.*

CU: Wade.

You learn how to act your place, son. This isn't Houston.

He stands and we follow him toward the bar.

OTIS
(*voice-over*)
'Course I was young and full of beans then –

The camera passes Wade and instead of Minnie there stands Otis, in the present day, reminiscing. We are back in '95.

– didn't understand the spot I was putting Roderick in.

SAM
And that was the last time you saw him?

We shift to see Sam sitting where Wade was headed.

OTIS
Oh – I think he came in one more time with Hollis and – naw, your Daddy wasn't with them. Made their monthly pickup. Roderick wasn't in so I just kept my mouth good and shut and handed over that envelope.

SAM
That was the night he disappeared?

OTIS
(*shakes his head*)
Could of been. That was white people's business.

SAM
And when my father was Sheriff?

OTIS
What about it?

SAM
What was your deal with him?

Otis smiles, chooses his words carefully.

OTIS
Buddy was more a part of the big picture – county political machine, chamber of commerce, zoning board – if I kept those people happy, he was pretty much on my side.
(*smiles*)
Whenever somebody thought they start up another bar for the

black folks, they'd be – how should I put this? They'd be officially discouraged.

SAM

He ever accept cash for a favor?

Otis smiles, looks away to ponder his response.

OTIS

I don't recall a prisoner ever died in your father's custody. I don't recall a man in this town – black, white, Mexican – who'd hesitate a minute before they'd call on Buddy Deeds to solve a problem. More than that I wouldn't like to say.

INT. CAR – LATE AFTERNOON

Pilar drives Amado and her daughter Paloma home.

AMADO

If you had your way I wouldn't have any friends.

PILAR

Oh, come on, Amado –

AMADO

Just 'cause I'm not like Little Miss Honor Roll here –

PILAR

Leave your sister out of it.

AMADO

You and all of the teachers in this dump – your story's over, so you don't want anybody else to have fun.

We see on Pilar's face that this has scored.

PALOMA

You jerk –

AMADO

I'm not talking to you. You don't have any friends.

Pilar eases the car down San Jacinto Street, seeing something on the street and tuning her kids' conversation out.

PALOMA

Who'd want to be friends with that bunch of *pachuco* wannabes?

AMADO

I don't pretend I came over on the Mayflower.

PALOMA

And those stupid girls who hang out with them –

AMADO

Just shut up.

Pilar's POV: Sam. Sam walks on the sidewalk parallel to them, talking with three other Men.

PALOMA
(*off-screen*)

Joanie Orozco's telling the whole school she's like desperately in love with Santo Guerra.

AMADO
(*off-screen*)

So?

PALOMA
(*off-screen*)

It's pathetic. You can't be desperately in love when you're fourteen years old.

Pilar is still looking fixedly out the window.

Not if you have half a brain in your head.

PILAR

Of course you can.

PALOMA

What?

PILAR

It doesn't have anything to do with being smart.

EXT. SAN JACINTO STREET – LATE AFTERNOON

Danny Padilla is arguing with H. L. Briggs, a construction company big shot, and Jorge Guerra, a Council member in his forties, and Sam, as they walk down the sidewalk of the main street.

JORGE
What I'm saying is, I don't see the point. You had your chance when the dedication committee was meeting –

DANNY
I've got new information –

H. L.
It's ancient goddam history, Danny –

DANNY
1963, they dam up the north branch to make Lake Pescadero. A whole little town disappears –

H. L.
A squatter town –

DANNY
People had been living in Perdido for over a hundred years. Mexicans and Chicanos are deported, evicted, moved forcibly out of their houses by our local hero, Buddy Deeds, and his department –

JORGE
There was a bill from the State Legislature –

DANNY
Families were split apart, a whole community was destroyed –

H. L.
They were trespassing, Danny –

DANNY
– and who ends up with lakefront property bought for a fraction of the market price? Buddy Deeds, Sheriff of Rio County, and his Chief Deputy, Hollis Pogue.

They all look at Sam, who has been listening patiently the whole while. They've reached his office.

155

SAM

You finished?

DANNY

Look, I'm not after you, Sam. I just think people in town ought to know the full story on Buddy Deeds.

SAM
(*nods*)

That makes two of us.

Sam steps into his office, leaving H. L. shaking his head.

H. L.

You best be thankful that's the son and not the father. Buddy woulda kicked your ass from here to sundown.

INT. HALLWAY – DEL'S HOUSE – LATE AFTERNOON

We track down a hallway as Celie walks toward us, calling ahead. Chet stands in the middle of the hall behind her.

CELIE

I don't see what the big deal is. Go back over, talk to the man and bury the hatchet.

DEL
(*off-screen*)

Why should I be the one? He had almost forty years, I didn't hear a word from him.

CELIE

He was probably embarrassed –

Celie passes us and Del crosses back in the other direction from behind the camera, carrying boxes of their belongings. We continue our slow track forward.

DEL

Otis Payne was never embarrassed about a thing in his life.

CHET

Dad –

CELIE
(*off-screen*)
Del, you were eight years old when he left –

DEL
He didn't *leave*, he moved three houses down with one of my mother's best friends.

CHET
Dad –?

DEL
'Hey, Delmore, where's your Daddy?'

Del disappears into the bedroom at the end of the hall.

(*off-screen*)
That godforsaken town, everybody into everybody else's business. And everybody loved Big O –

Del comes back out, empty-handed.

Big O was always there with a smile or a loan or a free drink.

CHET
Dad, can I talk to you about track?

CELIE
(*off-screen*)
People change.

DEL
Not that much.

CHET
Dad, I talked to the track coach –

DEL
I thought we already had this out? Next year, if your grades are high enough –

CHET
I have a B average.

DEL

How many B-average students do you think they take at West Point?

CELIE
(*off-screen*)
Well, we're stuck here for three years, we're going to have to see him –

DEL

No, we don't.

Del steps away past us, leaving Chet, defeated.

INT. CAFÉ – NIGHT

We start on Enrique, talking surreptitiously on the pay phone on the way to the kitchen.

ENRIQUE
Sábado por la noche – Sí, es el más seguro – Voy a cruzar por la mañana, y pues tendremos que esperar – [Friday night – Yes, that's the safest – I'll cross in the morning and then we'll have to wait –]

Mercedes bustles by, snapping her fingers.

MERCEDES

Off the phone, Enrique, we've got people waiting. *Andale!*

We follow Mercedes back into the kitchen, where she moves through, kibbitzing the operation.

WAITRESS
(*off-screen*)
Necesito las chuletas! [I need pork chops!]

COOK
(*off-screen*)
Listos! (Ready!)

Mercedes stops by a Young Girl prepping a pork loin to be cooked. She isn't wearing gloves.

MERCEDES
Dónde están sus guantes? Tonta! Quiere matar a mis clientes?
[Where are your gloves? Stupid! You want to kill my
customers?]

*She continues past, shaking her head, bringing us to Pilar, who is trying
to stay out of the way.*

These ones coming up are getting stupider every year.

PILAR
Maybe you're just getting less patient.

MERCEDES
If they're going to survive here, they have to know how to
work. *Flaco! Adelante! Los clientes esperan!*

PILAR
Well, you hire illegals –

MERCEDES
(*indignant*)
Nobody is illegal in my café! They've got green cards, they've
got relatives who were born here – if they only had a little
common sense I'd be very happy.

PILAR

If you spent a little more time training them –

MERCEDES

Did you come here to tell me how to run my business?

PILAR

No. I was wondering if you'd like to take a trip down south
with us. Maybe see where you grew up –

MERCEDES

Why would I want to go there?

PILAR

Oh, come on – you must be curious how it's changed. Amado
is into this big Tejano roots thing and I've never been further
than Ciudad León –

MERCEDES

You want to see Mexicans, open your eyes and look around
you. We're up to our ears in them.

*Pilar gives up on the trip. She watches her mother poking at the plates
of chips and salsa ready to go out.*

PILAR

Mami, how old were you when my father –

MERCEDES

He was killed.

PILAR

Right. When he was killed.

MERCEDES

A little older than Paloma is now.

PILAR

How come you never got married again?

Mercedes just glares at her.

There must have been somebody.

MERCEDES
(*mutters*)

I was too busy.

PILAR

Nobody's too busy.

MERCEDES

Maybe now. It was different back then. I had this place, I was doing all the shopping, all the cooking – what do I need some *chulo* with grease under his nails to drink up the profit?

PILAR
(*pissed off*)

Thank you.

MERCEDES

I don't mean Fernando.

PILAR

Mami, the first time I brought him home, those were your exact words – 'some *chulo* with grease under his nails' –

MERCEDES

I never said that.

PILAR

You made it pretty damn clear you thought he was nobody.

MERCEDES

I felt that you could do better for yourself –

PILAR

What? Become a nun? You didn't want me going out with Anglos –

MERCEDES

I never said that. It was just that boy –

PILAR

'That boy' – Mami, say his name for chrissakes!

The Employees are staring. Mercedes won't look at her daughter as she steps out of the kitchen, banging into Enrique on his way back in.

MERCEDES

You people are stealing my money – *Entiende? Robándome!*

Mercedes is gone. The Young Girl, pulling plastic gloves on, looks to Pilar.

GIRL

Su madre? [Your mother?]

PILAR

Sí.

The Girl puts her hand on her heart in sympathy.

GIRL

Lo siento. [My condolences.]

INT. COUNTRY AND WESTERN BAR – NIGHT

A crowded room. C & W music plays on the box. Sam sits behind a bottle of beer as the bartender, Cody, in his early fifties, philosophizes.

CODY

Now I'm just as liberal as the next guy –

SAM

If the next guy's a redneck.

CODY

– but I gotta say I think there's something to this cold climate business. I mean, you go to the beach – what do you do? Drink a few beers, wait for a fish to flop up on the sand. Can't build no civilization that way. You got a hard winter coming, though, you got to plan ahead, and that gives your cerebral cortex a workout.

SAM

Good deal you were born down here, then.

CODY

You joke about it, Sam, but we are in a state of crisis. The lines of demarcation has gotten fuzzy – to run a successful civilization you got to have lines of demarcation between right and wrong, between this one and that one – your Daddy understood that. He was like the whatchacallit – the ref*ee* for this damn *menudo* we got down here. He understood how most people don't want their sugar and salt in the same jar.

SAM

You mixed drinks bad as you mix metaphors, you be out of a job.

CODY

Take that pair over in the corner –

Sam swivels to look where Cody points.

Place like this, twenty years ago. Buddy woulda been *on* them two –

Sam's POV: corner booth. Cliff and Priscilla talk across the table.

(*off-screen*)

He would of went over there and give them a warning. Not 'cause he had it in for the colored –

On Sam and Cody.

– but just as a kind of safety tip.

SAM

Yeah. I bet he would.

CODY

Old Sam *stood* for somethin', you know? The day that man died they broke the goddam mold.

On booth – Cliff and Priscilla. Things are obviously more than professional between these two.

PRISCILLA

So where does that put us?

CLIFF

Well – I don't see what's changed. No PDAs, no necking on the obstacle course –

PRISCILLA

Seriously.

                    CLIFF
Seriously, I think we should get married.

                    PRISCILLA
We been through this before –

                    CLIFF
We should just do it.

                    PRISCILLA
And if I get a shot at a promotion somewhere –

                    CLIFF
You could take it –

                    PRISCILLA
It's up or out these days, Cliff. Say I get transferred to a
different post –

                    CLIFF
I'd quit the Army for you, if it came to that.

                    PRISCILLA
                    (*grins*)
Man's gonna retire in two years and he offer to quit. Big
goddam deal.

                    SAM
                    (*off-screen*)
Excuse me –

They look up to see Sam standing over them.

                    CLIFF
Sheriff – hi – this is Sergeant – this is Priscilla Worth –

                    SAM
Pleased to meet you.

                    CLIFF
Sheriff Deeds was in on our archeological find yesterday.

                    PRISCILLA
It true they gonna build a shopping mall out there?

SAM

If certain people have their way, it's going to be a new jail.

PRISCILLA

Damn. Maybe we got in the wrong business. They closin'
down military left and right, puttin' up jails like 7–11 stores.

SAM

Do either of you have any idea when they stopped using that
site as a rifle range?

CLIFF

They stopped training infantry there in the late fifties. It was
just a playground for the jackrabbits till they gave it to the
county last year.

PRISCILLA

You know who it was they dug up?

SAM

Not for sure yet. But I kind of wish they hadn't.

EXT. CAFÉ – NIGHT

*Enrique steps out of the darkened café, followed by Mercedes, who locks
up. Mercedes steps over to an expensive-looking car.*

ENRIQUE

Es muy lindo, su coche –

MERCEDES

En inglés, Enrique. This is the United States. We speak
English.

ENRIQUE

Is very beautiful, your car.

MERCEDES

Good night, Enrique.

She slides into the car.

ENRIQUE

Buenas noches, Señora Cruz.

Enrique walks in the opposite direction.

FADE OUT

EXT. BIG O'S ROADHOUSE – DAY

CU: Del, in uniform, approaches the front door of Big O's, not open for business yet. We tighten as he stops to read a handlettered sign next to it: 'BLACK SEMINOLE EXHIBIT – REAR ENTRANCE'. *He steps in.*

INT. ROADHOUSE – DAY

Late-fifties R & B plays on the jukebox. Otis stands behind the counter hooking the beer taps up. Del steps in and sits on a stool at the far end of the bar, tense, looking around the place. When Otis sees him, he stops dead. They lock eyes for a moment, then Otis turns to call.

> OTIS
> Carolyn – knock that off for a minute.

Carolyn Sykes, an attractive woman, maybe ten years younger than Otis, pulls the plug from the jukebox near where she's scrubbing bloodstains off the floor. She turns to look at the newcomer.

Del doesn't move to come closer.

> DEL
> Black Seminoles?

> OTIS
> (*shrugs*)
> Hobby of mine. Got some artifacts, couple pieces one of your men out at the base made. Free admission.

Del nods toward where Carolyn is mopping.

> DEL
> That where he was shot?

> OTIS
> That's where he fell.

> DEL
> You get much of that in here?

OTIS

It's a bar. People come together, drink, fall in love, fall out of love, air their grudges out –

DEL

Deal drugs in the bathroom –

OTIS

If I thought it would help I'd put up a sign telling them not to. Right under the one about the employees washing their hands.

Carolyn has come over by Otis, lugging the bucket and mop.

This here's Carolyn. Honey, this is my son, Delmore.

DEL

Nice to meet you, ma'am.

Carolyn nods, shoots a look to Otis.

CAROLYN

I'll be in back waiting for that delivery.

They wait till she is gone to start again.

OTIS

So.

DEL

So tell me why I shouldn't make this place off-limits.

OTIS

This is an official visit, then –

DEL

I assume a lot of your business is from our people.

Otis pulls a tap back and it coughs before squirting beer.

OTIS

Your boys out there cooped up together, need somewhere they can let the steam out. If they're black, there's not but one place in this town they feel welcome. Been that way since before you were born.

167

DEL

We have an enlisted man's club at the post.

OTIS

Well, you're the Man out there now, aren't you? It's your call.

DEL

That's right.

OTIS
(*smiles*)

I been hearing rumors about this new commander coming for a couple weeks now. Boys say they heard he's a real hard case. Spit-and-polish man. Full-bird colonel name of Payne, they say. Bet you never figured you end up back here.

DEL

The Army hands you a command, you go wherever it is.

OTIS

Right.

DEL

I hear things, too. People call you the Mayor of Darktown.

OTIS
(*shrugs*)

Over the years, this is the one place that's always been there. I loan a little money out, settle some arguments. Got a cot in the back – people get afraid to go home they can spend the night. There's not enough of us to run anything in this town – the white people are mostly out on the lake now and the Mexicans hire each other. There's the Holiness Church and there's Big O's place.

DEL

And people make their choice –

OTIS
(*smiles*)

A lot of 'em choose both. There's not like a borderline between the good people and the bad people – you're not either on one side or the other –

Del looks away, not wanting to believe this.

> (*softly*)
> I gonna meet that family of yours?

DEL
Why would you want to do that?

OTIS
Because I'm your father.

Del gives him a dark look and lets the statement hang between them. He gets up and heads for the door.

DEL
You'll get official notification when I make my decision.

He is out the door. Otis pulls himself a beer as Carolyn steps back out.

CAROLYN
So that's him –

OTIS
Yeah – that's him. Got two, three thousand people under him out there, you count the civilians.

CAROLYN
That must be a laugh a minute.

EXT. SAN JACINTO STREET – DAY

Sam walks down the main street of town. A crowd is gathering at the other end for the ceremony.

H. L.
(*off-screen*)

Sheriff!

We widen as H. L. and Jorge catch up to him. H. L. slaps Sam on the back.

H. L.
Historic occasion, isn't it?

SAM
Seems like we have another one every week.

H. L.

Jorge and his Chamber of Commerce boys got to keep things hummin' –

JORGE

We're building up tourism, Sam –

SAM

People come here to catch bass and to get laid at the Boy's Town in Cuidad León –

JORGE

Sam –

SAM

You ought to put up a banner – 'Frontera, Texas: Gateway to Cut-Rate Pussy' –

H. L.

That kind of talk doesn't help, Sam.

SAM

Rather have that than the ten-foot-high catfish statue –

JORGE

I got Eddie Richter at the *Sentinel* to kill that story.

SAM

The Perdido thing?

JORGE

He agreed it wasn't exactly news –

SAM

Danny's gonna be out for blood the next time.

H. L.

Which is why we need to talk to you about the new jail – just so we're all on the same page.

SAM

We don't need a new jail.

H. L.

That's a matter of interpretation –

SAM

We're already renting cells to the Feds for their overflow –

JORGE

There was a mandate in the last election.

SAM

It wouldn't happen to be your construction company gonna get the bid on building this thing, would it, H. L.? And Jorge, you wouldn't be thinking about a couple dozen new jobs to dangle in front of the voters –

H. L.

Dammit, Sam, the people are concerned about *crime* –

SAM

We need a drug rehab program, we need a new elementary school –

JORGE

There isn't money allocated for that. But a jail –

SAM

Look, I'm not gonna campaign against your deal here, but if anybody asks me, I got to tell them the truth. We – don't – need a new – *jail*.

H. L.

When we backed you –

SAM

When you backed me you needed somebody named Deeds to bump the other fella out of office. Hey, folks –

Sam and the others smile as they reach the crowd of Townspeople, mostly small business owners and retired people. Photographers from the paper and a local TV News Crew wait by a veiled statue roped off in a little traffic island. Mercedes, dressed to kill, stands waiting next to Hollis with a huge pair of scissors in her hand.

CU: Mercedes slowly working the blades of the scissors. She looks coldly at Sam.

CU: Sam. He nods to her as the crowd opens a path for him.

Let's get this thing over with.

INT. MIKEY'S WORKSHOP – MORNING

We start on a two-foot-high statue of a cowboy made from old bullets and shell casings. We pan past a few others, the poses lifted from Frederic Remington paintings, till we see Mikey, gluing together a work in progress, a Remington book propped open in front of him. Cliff sits at the worktable playing absently with the old bullets spilled out from Mikey's bag.

MIKEY

Never thought I'd see the day a buddy of mine was dating a woman with three up and three down on her shoulder.

CLIFF

I think it's beyond what you'd call dating.

MIKEY

You going to get married?

CLIFF
(*shrugs*)

Maybe.

MIKEY

You met her family? They gonna be cool about you being a white guy?

CLIFF

Priscilla says they think any woman over thirty who isn't married must be a lesbian. She figures they'll be so relieved I'm a man –

MIKEY

Always heartwarming to see a prejudice defeated by a deeper prejudice. But marriage, man – I did two tours in Southeast Asia and I was married for five years – I couldn't tell you which experience was worse.

Cliff picks up a slug.

CLIFF

Hey, Mikey –

MIKEY

I knew she was Japanese going into it, but she didn't tell me
the ninja assassin part –

CLIFF

– Mikey.

MIKEY

Her parents acted like I was gonna blow my nose on their
curtains –

CLIFF

Mikey –

MIKEY

If I stayed out past ten with the guys she'd go into her Madam
Butterfly routine –

CLIFF

Mikey, look at this –

MIKEY

What – it's a bullet. I'm lousy with bullets here.

CLIFF

It's a .45.

MIKEY

Yeah?

CLIFF

This is the stuff we picked up the other day, right? The rest of
this is all .30 caliber –

MIKEY

They were using M-1s, yeah –

CLIFF

What's it doing on a rifle range?

Mikey holds the slug in front of his face –

MIKEY

We better call that Sheriff.

EXT. SAN JACINTO STREET – DAY

Hollis is finishing his oration, having put the crowd in a good mood.

> HOLLIS
> Sometime in the early seventies a reporter from a national magazine was talking to the governor of our Lone Star state, and he asked him, 'Governor, what's your ideal of what a real Texan ought to be?' Governor said, 'That's easy, son – you just do down to Rio County and get a look at Sheriff Buddy Deeds.'

Applause.

Sam watching the crowd.

Sam's POV: we pan with his gaze across smiling faces, till he comes to Danny and a couple of Chicano friends, looking grim. We rack focus beyond them to see Pilar, watching the ceremony from a few yards back.

> (off-screen)
> Thank you. We've got one more person to hear from –

On Hollis.

> – and he's somebody who probably knew Buddy better than any of us. Sam – would you say a few words?

Sam is not thrilled to be called on. He steps forward reluctantly to applause.

> SAM
> You folks who remember my father knew him as Sheriff. But at home he was also judge, jury –

He looks to Hollis.

> – and executioner.

Laughter. Sam holds Hollis's eyes for a moment before continuing.

> This is a real honor you're doing him today, and if Buddy was around I'm sure his hat size would be gettin' bigger every minute.

On Pilar watching.

(*off-screen*)

I used to come to this park to hide from him. Now that you're putting his name on it –

On Sam.

I'll have to find someplace new to duck out.

More laughter.

I do appreciate it, and wherever he is, Buddy's puttin' the beer on ice for the bunch of you. Thank you.

Applause. Sam steps back and Mercedes steps forward with her scissors without looking at him.

HOLLIS

And now my fellow Council member and one of Frontera's most respected businesswomen, Mrs Mercedes Cruz, will do the honors for us –

Mercedes freezes, smiling, till the Still Photographers have gotten their shots, then snips the cord to a pulley system that lets the cloth drop.

On statue: the cloth drops to reveal a bas-relief in brass set in a block of smooth limestone. A decent likeness of Buddy in uniform, his hand on the shoulder of a small Chicano-looking boy who stands beside him, eyes raised worshipfully. Applause from the gathering.

Sam watching, a bit removed, as Mercedes shakes hands with Jorge and H. L. and Hollis for the cameras. He overhears a pair of Bystanders who are checking out the statue.

BYSTANDER 1

(*off-screen*)

It does look like old Buddy.

BYSTANDER 2

(*off-screen*)

I think he's gonna run that Mexican kid in for loiterin' –

The Bystanders laugh. Sam steps away, intercepting Mercedes as she steps away.

SAM

Nice to see you, Mrs Cruz.

Mercedes just looks at him, keeps going. His gaze brings him to Pilar, standing on the sidewalk, watching. Sam steps over from the dispersing crowd.

Field trip?

PILAR

Lunch hour. My next class isn't till nine-thirty.

SAM

Want to take a walk?

EXT. RIVERSIDE – DAY

Sam and Pilar walk together alongside the Rio.

SAM

Your mother still doesn't like me.

PILAR

I can't name anybody she does like these days.

176

SAM

I see she built a place up here by the river.

PILAR

A real palace. She rattles around alone in that thing –

SAM

She's done well for herself – on her own and all –

PILAR

So she tells me three times a week.

She looks at Sam.

I thought you got through that pretty well.

SAM

They cooked the whole thing up without asking me.

PILAR

People liked him.

SAM

Most people did, yeah.

PILAR

I remember him watching me once. When I was little – before
you and I –

She shrugs.

I was on the playground with all the other kids, but I thought
he was only looking at me. I was afraid he was going to arrest
me – he had those eyes, you know –

SAM

Yeah.

PILAR

Weird what you remember.

They walk in silence a moment.

SAM

Your boy, there –

PILAR

Amado.

SAM

Nice-looking kid.

PILAR

He hates me.

SAM

No –

PILAR

With Paloma, it's more like she pities and tolerates me –
totally age-appropriate. But Amado – he's – he's never been
book-smart. Had a hard time learning to read. Me being a
teacher and caring about those things is like an
embarrassment – like a betrayal.

SAM

Fernando did okay, and he dropped out –

PILAR

Fernando wasn't pissed off at everybody. He just wanted to
fix their cars.

SAM

It might just be the age. I spent my first fifteen years trying to
be just like Buddy and the next fifteen trying to give him a
heart attack.

Pilar looks at Sam.

PILAR

So why did you come back here, Sam?

SAM

Got divorced, I wasn't gonna work for my father-in-law
anymore. The fellas down here said they'd back me –

PILAR

You don't want to be Sheriff.

SAM

I got to admit it's not what I thought it'd be. Back when

178

Buddy had it – hell, I'm just a jailer. Run a sixty-room hotel with bars on the windows.

PILAR

It can happen so sudden, can't it? Being left out on your own.

SAM

You've got your mother, your kids –

PILAR

They've got me. Different thing.

They stop at a spot where you can climb down the bank.

SAM

Remember this?

Pilar looks at the spot. She isn't ready to deal with whatever memory it brings back.

PILAR

I should get back.

SAM

Pilar –

PILAR

Looks real bad if the teacher's late for class. It's really nice to talk with you, Sam.

She waves and walks away, feeling awkward. Sam watches for a minute, then turns and steps down to the bank. He looks at the water.

River surface. A little piece of tree bark is tossed onto the water and drifts away with the current. We tilt up to see Young Pilar tossing bark into the river as Young Sam sits on the bank beside her. They are fourteen and fifteen years old.

It is 1972.

YOUNG SAM

You going to tell her?

YOUNG PILAR

You going to tell him?

YOUNG SAM

He doesn't need to know all my business.

YOUNG PILAR

He's gonna find out.

YOUNG SAM

So? What's he gonna do, arrest us?

Young Pilar frowns, tosses more bark.

YOUNG PILAR

It's supposed to be some big sin, even if you love each other.

YOUNG SAM

You believe that?

CU: Young Pilar. She turns to look at Sam.

YOUNG PILAR

No.

We pan with her gaze to see Sam, present day, sitting on the bank, lost in thought.

SAM

Me neither.

EXT. ARMY POST – DAY

Athena walking between buildings, looking a bit out of it. Priscilla cuts into her.

PRISCILLA

Private Johnson!

ATHENA

Sergeant?

PRISCILLA

Report to Dr Innis at the clinic.

ATHENA

I'm feeling okay –

PRISCILLA

I'm very happy to hear that, Private. Now you go put some pee-pee in a cup for Dr Innis and I'll be feeling okay too.

ATHENA
(*reacts*)

You're testing me?

PRISCILLA

You and one hundred nineteen other fortunate individuals. Put it in gear.

ATHENA

Yes, Sergeant.

Priscilla watches Athena go, suspicious.

INT. SHERIFF'S OFFICE – AFTERNOON

Ray Hernandez and another Deputy guide Shadow back in from the courthouse in handcuffs.

RAY

Excellent performance, my friend. The judge was very impressed.

SHADOW

You don't need to cuff me.

RAY

You been talking so much trash today, you made us think you're a dangerous criminal. Be a good boy, now –

They guide him past Sam's desk.

SHADOW

You're the one who's a good boy. Man say 'fetch' and you fetch –

RAY

Just doing my job.

SHADOW

White man just using you to keep the black man down.

RAY

This isn't Houston, my friend. We pretty much running things now. Our good day has *come*.

SHADOW

You suckers haven't had a good day since the Alamo.

Ray smiles, pushes him out.

RAY

Andale, amigo.

We hold on Sam at his desk, tightening as he holds the .45 slug from the Sergeants in front of his eyes.

SAM

Lupe? Get me the Rangers up in Austin –

INT. MERCEDES'S KITCHEN – NIGHT

CU: glass. We hear old Mexican music. Ice cubes plunk into a glass.

Wider: Mercedes. Exhausted from a day at the café, she pours herself a Scotch and soda.

EXT. BACK PATIO – NIGHT

The back light is flicked on and Mercedes steps out with her drink in hand, the music audible from inside. She sinks into a recliner. We tighten as she closes her eyes. Something rustles out in the dark. Mercedes opens her eyes. There is whispering. Mercedes sits up and suddenly two Men run past the edge of the patio toward the front of the house. Mercedes sighs.

MERCEDES

Otra vez los mojados – [Wetbacks again –]

Mercedes searches to find a portable phone on the patio table, punches a number in.

Hello? Border Patrol?

EXT. SAM'S HOUSE – NIGHT

Sam, out of uniform, stands behind his little house chucking fallen pecans out into the dark, thinking, listening to the night sounds.

CU: Sam, working something out in his head. He looks off into the dark and we pan with his gaze.

A Man steps toward us, barely visible in the darkness. It is Charley Wade.

We're in Sam's revery, in 1957.

> WADE
> Who is that? Come out here where I can see you!

Blam! A gunshot, and Wade falls to his knees.

> You sonofabitch –

Wade falls on his face. A flashlight beam flicks on and plays over his body. We pan back along the beam to see Buddy, holstering his pistol. He hears something, swings the flashlight up.

On Sam. We are back in 1995. Sam is blasted in the face with a flashlight beam.

> PATROLMAN
> (*off-screen*)
> Hold it right there! *Brazos arriba!*

Sam, squinting toward the light to see who it is, raises his arms over his head.

> ZACK
> (*off-screen*)
> Get that thing off 'im! He's one of ours –

> SAM
> Zack?

The flashlight beam pans away and Zack Pollard, a Border Patrol agent, steps out of the dark to Sam.

> ZACK
> Hey. Sam. Sorry 'bout that.

> SAM
> What's up?

ZACK

We had about a dozen wets come over just upriver. They ran into one of our posts – it was like a breakshot on a pool table, illegals runnin' every which way –

SAM

I haven't seen anybody come by.

ZACK

We'll get 'em.
(*looking around*)
So you livin' out here now?

SAM

Yeah. It's quiet –

ZACK

I heard about that deal for your father. You must be real proud.

SAM

Sure.

ZACK

The stories people tell, he was a real colorful fella.

PATROLMAN
(*off-screen*)

Zack! We got one!

ZACK

Well – back on the clock. You see any of our neighbors from the south, let 'em know I'm lookin' for 'em.

SAM

'Night.

Zack steps away. Sam shakes the pecans still in his hand, goes back to chucking them.

EXT. COURTYARD – NIGHT

Older Chicano couples dance to Mexican music playing from speakers set up in the apartment complex courtyard. We tilt up to see Enrique watching from his window.

INT. APARTMENT – NIGHT

Enrique steps away from the window, music still blasting in, and sits on the bed of his drab furnished apartment. He goes back to tying knots in a length of clothesline, splicing it to another. On the bed beside him are two new flashlights and the batteries, still in their packaging. He begins to coil the rope – it is hundreds of feet long.

EXT. FRONT PORCH, PILAR'S HOUSE – NIGHT

Pilar sits on her front porch, listening to the music in the distance. A woman singing a Mexican love ballad. After a while we hear Paloma open the screen door behind her.

> PALOMA
> (*off-screen*)

Mom?

> PILAR

Yeah?

> PALOMA
> (*off-screen*)

You gonna stay out here?

> PILAR

For a while.

A silence. They listen to the record.

> PALOMA
> (*off-screen*)

What's she singing about?

> PILAR
> (*smiles*)

What do you think?

FADE OUT

INT. SHERIFF'S OFFICE – EARLY MORNING

Sam has been up since dawn, searching through piles of old department records. Papers cover his desk and the chairs he's dragged over next to it. He reads out loud to himself from a report in front of him.

185

SAM

First bullet entered beneath the left eye, severing optical nerve
and exiting from top rear of skull causing tissue damage –

*Documents – various shots. As Sam reads, we see quick pops of various
records:*

Certificates of death.

An old Sheriff's Department payroll.

An autopsy report.

Eviction notices.

(*off-screen*)
– and severe cerebral hemorrhaging. Second bullet entered
left cheek driving fragment of upper and lower molars into
base of skull. Third bullet –

Real estate transfers.

A map of the proposed Lake Pescadero.

Another autopsy report.

A fax copy of the forensics dental report on Charley Wade.

Another autopsy report.

CU: Sam, intent as he pores over the paperwork.

On Legal pad. We tilt down to read various notes Sam has written.

Reynaldo Garcia killed by Shf Wade – 3/49

Hollis Kinney hired by Shf Dep. – 9/51

Lucas Johnson k. by Shf Wade – 7/53

Horace Gaines k. by Shf Wade – 1/54

Santiago Huerta k. by Shf Wade – 4/54

Rifle range closed – 9/56

Eladio Cruz k. by Shf Wade – 12/56

Buddy Deeds hired by Shf Dep. – 2/57

Shf Wade disappears – 3/57 $10,000 cnty funds missing – Buddy Deeds new Shf

We come to Sam's hand, writing. When it clears we can read the last entry.

Mercedes Cruz hired as cook, Rio Co. jail – 4/57 ?????

CU: Sam trying to put it all together. Pete Zayas, a skinny, older man in trustee's coveralls, wanders in, emptying the trash baskets in the front office.

> PETE

Morning, Sheriff.

> SAM

Hey, Pete. How's it going?

> PETE

Time marches on.

> SAM

How much you got left?

> PETE

Three months.

> SAM

You stop growing that loco weed at your place, you'd see a lot more daylight.

> PETE

It was for personal consumption.

> SAM

You're going to smoke an acre and a half of marijuana?

> PETE

I got a bad stomach. It helps me digest.

Pete dumps out the basket by Sam.

Your father never bothered me about it. Leastways not till the drug people got on his back in the late sixties.

SAM

I thought he busted you a couple times.

PETE

Different charge. I had a still. Made my own mescal.

Sam looks up at him.

That's how I ruined my stomach.

SAM
(*smiles*)
I'm surprised he bothered with it.

PETE

He was afraid I was going to poison somebody. Your father
tried to do good for people –

SAM

So I've heard –

PETE

And your mother was a saint. That summer I built the patio
at your house? She made me lunch every day.

SAM

Well, you were working there –

PETE

It could have just been a box lunch from the jail.

Sam looks up again, troubled.

SAM

You built our patio while you were on the county?

PETE

Out in the fresh air, nice gringo lady making you pies – who's
gonna sit back in a little jail cell all day? Sheriff Buddy, man.
Como él no hay dos. And after that *cabrón* Charley Wade –

SAM

I've heard Wade was a bit tough on the Mexicans –

PETE

He murdered Eladio Cruz. That tough enough for you?

                    SAM

Murdered him?

                    PETE

Chucho Montoya saw it with his own eyes. Shot him in cold
blood.

EXT. SAN JACINTO STREET — MORNING

*Ray Hernandez, heading in to work, comes upon Sam getting into his
car.*

                    RAY

You're out early.

                    SAM

Yeah.

                    RAY

Haven't seen much of you at the jail lately.

                    SAM

I been working on a few things.

                    RAY

Uh-huh.

                    SAM

I'm going over to the other side.

                    RAY
                  (*concerned*)

The Republicans?

                    SAM

No – to Mexico. I've got to talk to somebody.

                    RAY

They got telephones.

                    SAM

Gotta be in person.

                    RAY

Oh.

An awkward silence. Sam sits into the driver's seat and Ray leans down to talk.

Sam? I – the Committee – you know Jorge and H. L. and all – they asked me –

SAM

They want you to stand for Sheriff next election.

RAY

Yeah.

SAM

You'd do a good job.

RAY

How 'bout you?

SAM

Don't know if I'll still want it.

RAY

I didn't want to be going around your back.

SAM

I appreciate you telling me.

Sam looks at his Chief Deputy.

You think we need a new jail?

RAY

Well, it's a complicated issue –

Sam smiles, turns the engine on.

SAM

Yeah, Ray, you'd be a hell of a Sheriff.

EXT. SCHOOL – MORNING

Pilar sits with Amado on the football field bleachers before school starts.

PILAR

I'm only going to have you for two more years. If you decide not to go on to college –

AMADO

I can't take any more school.

PILAR

– you're going to be on your own.

AMADO

So?

PILAR

So I'm worried about you. I don't want you to end up in jail like your friends.

AMADO

They're not going to jail.

PILAR

Don't try to con me, Amado. You knew how they got all those things.

AMADO

Just some rich Anglo out on the lake. Don't even live here all year.

PILAR

That makes it okay?

AMADO

They stole our land –

PILAR

Save your breath. That line doesn't cut it with me.

silence. Amado sulks.

How do you think you're going to make a living?

AMADO

I can fix cars.

PILAR

You can fix old cars. Mr Washburn told me that the cars they're making now are all computerized –

AMADO

You think I can't learn that?

PILAR

I think you can learn whatever you want to. I just don't see you doing it. If you want to settle for –

AMADO

I'm not settling for anything. I like cars. It's just not a move up the ladder to you, so you think it's a waste.

PILAR

That isn't true.

AMADO

Oh, come on – you and Grandma think anybody who works with their hands is a peasant. When Dad –

PILAR

If you grew up to be anywhere near as good a man as your father was, I would be happy! I would be thrilled.

They look at each other for a long moment.

AMADO

It's my life. If I want to fuck it up, that's my business.

PILAR
(*nods*)

I said pretty much the same thing to my mother when I was your age.

AMADO

And what did she do?

PILAR

Two years at hard labor, Our Lady of Perpetual Help.

AMADO

Catholic school. Nasty.

Pilar is nearly in tears.

PILAR

Honey, I think you're smart and you're good and I love you. So don't act like an idiot, all right?

EXT. BORDER CROSSING – DAY

We see Sam's car roll through the 'express lane' as other cars in both directions stop by the inspection booths. Sam drives across the bridge over the Rio.

EXT. STREETS – CIUDAD LEÓN

Sam drives slowly through the sprawling, more populous town on the other side. Lots of the streets are unpaved. We pan with the car till we hold on Anselma, a country girl of fifteen, aimlessly walking the streets.

EXT. LLANTERIA (TIRE REPAIR SHOP) – DAY

We watch a Kid about Amado's age pulling a tire off its rim to put a patch on it.

> CHUCHO
> (*off-screen*)
> Over here we don't throw everything away like you gringos do.

Chucho and Sam.

Chucho Montoya, in his mid-fifties, stands by Sam drinking a Coke as they watch the Kid work.

> Recycling, right? We invented that. The Government doesn't have to tell people to do it.

> SAM
> You own this place?

> CHUCHO
> This place, the one across the street, four other ones around Ciudad León – *soy el Rey de las Llantas.* King of the Tires. Lots of your people rollin' back over that bridge on my rubber.

> SAM
> (*nods*)
> You lived in the States for a while?

CHUCHO

Fifteen years in El Paso.

SAM

Made some money, came back here –

CHUCHO

Something like that.

SAM

You ever know a fella named Eladio Cruz?

Chucho smiles, draws a line in the dirt with his heel.

CHUCHO

You the Sheriff of Rio County, right? *Un jefe muy respetado.*
Step over this line –

Sam obliges.

Ay, qué milagro! You're not the sheriff of nothing anymore –
just some *tejano* with a lot of questions I don't have to answer.

Sam smiles, plays with the line with his toe.

Bird flying south – you think he sees that line? Rattlesnake,
javelina – whatever you got – halfway across that line they
don't start thinking different. So why should a man?

SAM

Your government always been pretty happy to have that line.
The question's just been where to *draw* it –

CU: Chucho.

CHUCHO

My government can go fuck itself, and so can yours. I'm
talking about people here – men. *Mi amigo* Eladio Cruz is
giving some friends of his a lift in his *camión* one day –

We pan from Chucho to the flat tire on a battered old pickup truck.

(*voice-over*)
– but because he's on one side of this invisible line and not
the other, they got to hide in the back like criminals –

Eladio Cruz, young and good-looking, squats into the shot to examine the tire, jack in hand.

It is 1956.

And because over there he's just another Mex *bracero*, any man with a badge is his *jefe* –

Conjunto music comes from the truck radio. Young Chucho steps past Eladio.

> ELADIO
>
> *Dónde vas, Chucho? Tienes que quedar escondido!* [Shit, Chucho, you got to stay hidden!]

> YOUNG CHUCHO
>
> *Voy a romper las riñones si no hago pipi –* [I'm gonna bust my kidneys if I don't pee –]

We track back with Young Chucho to see we are at the side of a dirt road on the scrubby flatland near the border. Eladio's battered pickup truck has wood-slat sides and a canvas top. Eladio begins to undo the nuts on the flat tire as Young Chucho climbs down into a dry creek bed to relieve himself.

> *Los demás son tan espantados que prefieran mojar sus pantalones.* [The other guys are so scared they'd rather wet their pants.]

Chucho tightens as he sees something, ducks down.

> *Mira, Eladio!* [Look!]

We pan to see the Sheriff's car approaching in a cloud of dust.

Eladio calls from where he lies changing the tire.

> ELADIO
>
> *Muchachos! Escóndases!* [Boys! Hide yourselves!]

INT. REAR OF TRUCK – DAY

Eight illegal Workers hear this and lie down, pulling a canvas tarp over themselves. We hear the car stop behind them.

EXT. ARROYO – DAY

CU: Chucho. He makes the sign of the cross as he presses his back against the dirt of the arroyo.

Sheriff Wade and Deputy Hollis get out of their car and start toward Eladio.

Eladio stands, takes a deep breath – Wade steps up to him with his hard-eyed smile.

> WADE
> *Hola, amigo. Problemas de llanta?* [Hey, friend. Tire problems?]

> ELADIO
> *No hay de qué. Tengo otra.* [No problem, I've got another.]

> WADE
> What's in the back?

EXT. TRUCK – DAY

Young Hollis strolls around the truck as if he's considering buying it. He reaches in and flicks the radio off.

> ELADIO
> Not much, *jefe.* Some watermelons.

> WADE
> I heard somebody been haulin' wets on this road.

> ELADIO
> I haven't seen anybody doing that.

> WADE
> This same person been bragging all over the county how he don't have to cut that big gringo Sheriff in on it – he can run his own operation 'thout any help. *Cómo se llama amigo?*

> ELADIO
> Eladio Cruz.

> WADE
> You know this road got a bad reputation, Eladio –

At the arroyo. Young Chucho peeks over the edge to see what's happening.

ELADIO

Reputation?

WADE

Bandidos, Injuns –

Closer: Men. Hollis wanders over to stand by Wade.

There's many an unfortunate soul been ambushed out on this stretch. Hope you're carrying some protection.

ELADIO

Protection?

WADE

You carryin' a firearm, son? Don't lie to me now.

ELADIO

Sí – tengo escopeto – just a shotgun –

WADE

Just a shotgun, huh? Better let me take a look at that.

Eladio opens the truck door and digs under the seat. Wade winks to Hollis, then turns and blam! *shoots Eladio through the head. Hollis jumps back, startled and horrified.*

YOUNG HOLLIS

Oh no – oh Jesus – oh my Lord –

WADE

Little greaser sonofabitch been running a goddam bus service. Think he can make a fool out of Charley Wade! Get them wets outta the back, Hollis, see what we've got –

CU: Chucho squatting in a ball to make himself as small as possible, eyes covered with his hands.

YOUNG HOLLIS
(*off-screen*)

You killed him –

WADE
(*off-screen*)
You got a talent for statin' the obvious, son. *Muchachos!*
Venga afuera! Brazos arribas! [Come on out! Hands up!]

Young Chucho hears footsteps approaching. We pan as he looks – a
man's boots appear at the top of the arroyo. We tilt up to see a sheriff,
backlit, then crane to see it is Sam, back in the present looking over the
site, troubled. His car sits on the empty road behind him. He frowns,
turns to go.

EXT. PARK – DAY

Somebody has spray-painted 'PERDIDO!' over the plaque of Buddy and
the little boy.

HOLLIS
(*off-screen*)
Hooligans –

Wider: Hollis and a couple of Men from the Public Works Department
look at the damage.

It happens again, we build a fence around it.

INT. CAFÉ – DAY

Enrique steels himself, trying to cover his nerves. We cross with him to a
booth.

ZACK
Podemos ganar muchas batallas pero la guerra ya es perdido –
[We can win a lot of battles but the war's already been
lost –]

Zack and another Border Patrolman look up at him.

CU: Enrique, eyes glued to his notepad.

ENRIQUE
You wan' something to drink?

EXT. ROADSIDE STAND – DAY

CU: cattle skull. A Georgia O'Keefe-looking cattle skull sits on a pedestal against the Western sky.

> WESLEY
> (*off-screen*)
> The longhorns go for ten times the price –

We widen as the skull is lifted by Wesley Birdsong, a Native American man in his seventies who wears extremely thick glasses. Sam tags along as the old man rearranges the display of Texas curios laid out in front of his trailer. Empty scrubland surrounds them.

> – but longhorns are hard to come by these days.

> SAM
> You sell much out here?

> WESLEY
> How am I gonna sell things if nobody comes by? This stretch of road runs between Nowhere and Nothin' Much.

> SAM
> Hell of a spot to put a business.

> WESLEY
> But you don't see much competition, do you?

He winks at Sam, picks up a wooden radio carved to resemble the Alamo.

> These things used to sell like hotcakes. Now, if it can't play those discs, they won't look at it.

He puts the radio down, looks out at the emptiness around.

> I like it here. Once I tried going onto that reservation to live. Couldn't take the politics. Damn Indians'll drive you crazy with that. Now your father – this wasn't what he had in mind at *all*. He come out of Korea, he had this Chevy with too much engine in it. He'd come roarin' up and down this road all hours of the day and night, looking for somebody to race.

He lifts a jar with a leathery brown thing in it.

Buffalo chips. Fella in Santa Fe told me he sells these as fast
as the buffalo can squeeze 'em out.

SAM

So when did Buddy leave?

WESLEY

For Frontera? Hell, I can't remember dates no more. I do
recall it was after an affair of the heart had gone sour on him.
He almost took some poor fella's head off at the Legion in
Arroyo Grande, and figured it was time to move on.

SAM

You think he killed anybody in Korea?

WESLEY

They don't hand those medals out for hidin' in your foxhole.
Would you buy this?

SAM

No –

WESLEY

Me neither.

He searches for something among the curios.

If he hadn't found that Deputy job, I believe Buddy might've
gone down the other path, got into some serious trouble.
Settled him right down. That and your mother. 'Course he
had that other one later.

SAM

Another woman?

WESLEY

Your mother wasn't one to get chased off her patch. Half the
damn county knew and nobody thought the worse of her for
seein' it through.

SAM

You know who it was?

WESLEY

The other one? Hell, at my age, every time you learn a new name you got to forget an old one. Your head's all crowded up – here it is –

Wesley stretches out a four-foot rattlesnake skin, rattles still attached.

This big fella was sleepin' in a crate at Cisco's junkyard right when I looked to see what was in it. Jumped up at my face – scared me so bad I killed him without thinkin'.

He shakes the rattles at Sam.

Gotta be careful where you're pokin' – who knows what you'll find.

INT. SCHOOL HALLWAY – DAY

Pilar talks with Molly as they near the administration office.

PILAR

I don't think you can take it personally –

MOLLY

I'd like to see them spend a day pulling fourteen-year-olds off of each other – I should get combat pay – I have new respect for some of my kids, meeting the parents they've been dealt –

Molly keeps going as Pilar ducks into the office.

PILAR

See you, Molly.

INT. OFFICE – DAY

Pilar crosses past the principal's secretary, Marisol.

MARISOL

Steve called for you.

PILAR

Steve?

MARISOL

Steve. Board of Education Steve who likes you? He goes for us hot-blooded Mexican girls, I can tell.

PILAR

Spanish, please. My mother would have a heart attack.

MARISOL

Your mother's family is Spanish?

PILAR

Sure, they go back to Cortez. When he rode by, they were squatting in a hut cooking hamsters for dinner.

MARISOL

You got to be interested in somebody, Pilar. All you do is work.

PILAR

All my mother does is work. That's how you get to be Spanish.

MARISOL

How 'bout the Sheriff?

PILAR

The Sheriff.

MARISOL

The old-high-school-heartthrob Sheriff. I thought you were crazy about each other. He's available, you're available –

PILAR

I'm unmarried. I'm not a*vail*able.

MARISOL

You told me one time it was true love.

Pilar takes the pile of mimeos and mail from her slot and turns to go.

PILAR
(*mutters*)
Nobody stays in love for twenty-three years.

EXT. DRIVE-IN MOVIE – NIGHT

It is 1972. An early-seventies cheesy action picture (Filipino women-in-chains or biker flick) is playing. We tilt down to a man's boots crunching across the gravel of the parking area. Now and then, the man turns a flashlight beam on a license plate. The cars are all pre-'72, lots of pickups, and the patrons are almost all teenagers. Some have turned their pickups around to sit on the tailgate and watch, while others have set lawn furniture out to sit on. We tilt up slightly to see the glint of a Rio County Sheriff's badge pinned on the man's shirt. He meets a deputy – Young Hollis coming in the other direction. Both train their flashlights on the license of the car we see in the background between them. We tilt and rack to see that nobody is visible through the window.

BUDDY
(*off-screen*)

Let's go.

We follow Buddy up to the driver's side of the car as Young Hollis goes to the passenger side. We pan with Buddy's hand down on the door handle – he grabs it, flings it open – the overhead light flicks on and there lie Young Sam and Pilar, teenagers, half their clothes off and just about to close the deal. Pilar screams and Young Hollis throws the door open by their heads.

Goddammit!

Buddy grabs Sam's ankles and yanks him out of the car onto the ground as the Deputy awkwardly pulls Pilar out the other side.

YOUNG SAM

What the hell are you doing? You fucking asshole!

BUDDY

How old is that girl? Goddammit, where's your goddam sense?

YOUNG PILAR
(*off-screen*)

Let me go! *Pendejo!*

YOUNG HOLLIS
(*off-screen*)
Come on now, Missy, get your clothes in order –

Sam is trying to kick and punch at his father, pausing in between to pull his pants up. People are booing and honking their horns all around.

YOUNG SAM
You got no fuckin' right! You stay out of my fuckin' life!

BUDDY
Gimme the keys – gimme the goddam car keys, son –

YOUNG HOLLIS
(*off-screen*)
What am I s'posed to do with her, Buddy?

BUDDY
You drive her home and tell her mother where we found her –

YOUNG PILAR
(*off-screen*)
Sam!

The kids are dragged forward into the headlights that are being turned on to see what the ruckus is. Both are crying, struggling.

YOUNG SAM
You leave her the fuck alone!

BUDDY
You just shut that filthy mouth, son. I'll deal with you when we get home –

YOUNG PILAR
Please, don't tell my mother! She's gonna kill me!

They step closer into the glaring headlights which white out the scene, then fade.

EXT. RUINED DRIVE-IN – DUSK

It is dusk, present day. Our eyes readjust to see Sam, standing by his car in the lot of the long-abandoned drive-in. The ruined screen rises in the background.

CU: Sam remembering. Music begins as he gets back into the car, pulls away.

Music continues as the car cruises out past the old marquee, a few letters still jumbled on it, several bullet holes around them.

INT. CAR – DUSK

Music continues as Sam drives, thinking.

EXT. ROADS – DUSK/NIGHT

Music continues as the car crosses the scrubland back toward town. Dusk turns to night.

EXT. PILAR'S HOUSE – NIGHT

Music continues as Sam cruises past Pilar's house. The car is not in the driveway. Paloma hangs out with a couple Friends under the porch light, laughing.

EXT. HIGH SCHOOL – NIGHT

Music continues as Sam's car pulls into the high school lot. He looks up toward the school.

EXT. WINDOW – NIGHT

Sam's POV. Music continues. We can see Pilar through the lighted window of her classroom, preparing something on the blackboard.

INT. CAR – NIGHT

Music ends as Sam leans back to wait.

EXT. PARKING LOT – NIGHT

Pilar digs in her bag for her car keys as she makes her way across the lot. She sees something, slows, reacting, then brings us to Sam in his car. He has parked head-to-foot next to hers. They look at each other for a long moment.

PILAR
(*softly*)

Follow me.

EXT. MAIN STREET – NIGHT

Nothing stirring. Pilar's car appears, closely followed by Sam's. The café has closed for the night.

INT. CAFÉ – NIGHT

Sam and Pilar sit on chairs next to each other, facing the window, talking softly. The streetlight shining through the letters in the front window makes patterns on their faces.

PILAR
We thought we were something, didn't we?

SAM
Yeah.

PILAR
I look at my kids in school – tenth, eleventh graders. That's who we were. Children.

SAM
Yeah.

PILAR
I mean what did we know about anything?

SAM
Nothing.

Pilar looks at him.

PILAR
When Nando died – it was so sudden – I was kind of in shock for a while. Then I woke up and there was the whole rest of my life and I didn't have any idea what to do with it.

SAM
You know the other day, you asked why I came back?

PILAR

Yeah?

SAM

I came back 'cause you were here.

Pilar nods. She gets up and we follow her across the dark room to the jukebox. She looks at the selections.

PILAR

My mother hasn't changed the songs since I was ten.

She puts in a quarter, punches some numbers. A Mexican ballad comes on. She crosses back to Sam, holds her hand out. He stands to greet her. They slow-dance in the empty café.

INT. SAM'S APARTMENT – BEDROOM

Sam and Pilar finish making love. They lie beside each other, shaking a little.

PILAR

Wow.

SAM

Yeah.

> PILAR

How come it feels the same?

> SAM

I don't know. It just feels good. Always did.

> PILAR

So what are we gonna do about this?

> SAM

More, I hope.

Pilar smiles, looks around the room.

> PILAR

How long have you lived here?

> SAM

Two years.

> PILAR

There's nothing on the walls. No pictures –

> SAM

Don't have kids. Other pictures – I don't know – it's nothing
I want to look back on.

> PILAR

Like your story is over.

> SAM

I've felt that way, yeah.

She puts her head on his chest.

> PILAR

It isn't. Not by a long shot.

Sam holds her and they lie silently for a moment.

> SAM

Pilar?

> PILAR

Yeah?

> SAM

What was your father's name?

> PILAR

Eladio. Eladio Cruz.

FADE OUT

EXT. PILAR'S HOUSE – MORNING

Paloma sits on the top step of the porch, reading teen magazines. Pilar steps out behind her, dressed casually, and squints at the day.

> PALOMA

She finally got up.

> PILAR

It's Saturday.

> PALOMA

You got in late last night.

> PILAR

Yeah. I had uhm – school business.

Paloma gives her a look, then holds a fashion page up for her to see.

> PALOMA

Can I get this?

> PILAR

Nobody really wears that stuff, Paloma.

> PALOMA

I could name five girls at school who have one just like it.

> PILAR

Enough with the clothes –

> PALOMA

Just 'cause you went to Catholic school and wore a uniform.

> PILAR

I only went for my last two years.

PALOMA

How come?

PILAR

Oh, my mother wanted to keep me away from a – away from boys.

Pilar steps out into the sun.

PALOMA

Did it work?

INT. CAFÉ – MORNING

Hollis is sitting alone in a booth, working on some huevos rancheros. Sam slides in across from him.

SAM

Morning, Hollis.

HOLLIS

Sam! Quite a do the other day. It meant a lot to folks that you said something.

SAM

You thought any more about our murder?

HOLLIS

We have a murder?

SAM

Charley Wade.

HOLLIS

I wish I could tell you I remembered something new, but I can't.

SAM

I got an idea what happened.

HOLLIS

Do you?

SAM

I think somewhere between Roderick Bledsoe's club and his

house, Wade ran into Buddy Deeds. I think Buddy put a bullet in him, waited for him to die, threw him in the trunk of the Sheriff's car and drove him out by the Army post. I think he buried him under four feet of sand and never looked back.

Hollis sits back to look Sam in the eye.

> HOLLIS
> You lived in the man's house what – seventeen, eighteen years? And you didn't get to know him any better than that?

> SAM
> I got to go see somebody in San Antonio today. Your memory gets any better, I'll be back tonight.

Sam stands and walks away. We hold on Hollis, his appetite gone.

EXT. BIG O'S – MORNING

Chet steps around to the side entrance.

INT. BLACK SEMINOLE EXHIBIT – DAY

CU: statue of a buffalo soldier made from spent bullets and shell casings, then pan to another, then widen to see Chet as he pokes his head in, bell of the door ringing. He steps in cautiously, looking around the room. On the walls there are photo-blowups, some artifacts, hand-lettered information on cardboard. Chet stops to look up at a picture of a bare-chested black man with a couple of feathers stuck in his headband.

> OTIS
> (*off-screen*)
> That's John Horse.

Chet turns to see Otis standing back by the door from the bar.

> Spanish in Florida called him Juan Caballo. John Horse.

> CHET
> (*looks at picture*)
> He a black man or an Indian?

OTIS
(*steps in*)

Both.

Otis crosses to the poker table, begins to clean up.

He was part of the Seminole Nation, got pushed down into the Everglades in pioneer days. African people who run off from the slaveholders hooked up with them, married up, had children. When the Spanish give up Florida, the US Army come down to move all them Indian peoples off to Oklahoma –

CHET

The Trail of Tears.

OTIS
(*smiles*)

They teaching that now? Good. Only a couple of 'em held out – this man, John Horse, and his friend Wild Cat, and a fella name of Osceola. Army put all of them in prison and Osceola died, but them other two escaped and put together a fighting band and held out another ten, fifteen years. Beat Zach Taylor and a thousand troops at Lake Okeechobee.

213

CHET

So they stayed in Florida?

OTIS

They got tired of fighting, went to the Indian Territories for a while. But the slave-raiders were on 'em even there, and one night they packed up and nearly the whole band rode down to Mexico. Crossed at Eagle Pass.

They move on to some photos of very African-looking people dressed in beautiful Seminole clothing.

Men worked for Santa Anna down there, waited out the Civil War. The land wasn't much to feed people on, so in 1870 they come north and put up at Fort Duncan and the men joined up what was called the Seminole Negro Indian Scouts. Best trackers either side of the border. Bandits, rustlers, Texas rednecks, Kiowa, Comanche.

CHET

They fought against the Indians?

OTIS

Same as they done in Mexico.

CHET

But they were Indians themselves.

OTIS

They were in the Army. Like your father.

CHET
(*surprised*)

You know who I am?

OTIS

I got a pretty good guess.

CHET

That guy who got shot –

OTIS

You didn't go telling your father you were here?

CHET

Are you kidding? And face a court-martial?

OTIS
(*smiles*)
He's a pretty tough old man, huh?

CHET

No sports if I don't keep a B average, no TV on school nights, no PDAs –

OTIS

PDA?

CHET

Public Display of Affection. Every time he moves up a rank, it's like he's got to tighten the screws a little more –

OTIS

Well –

CHET

I mean, just 'cause he didn't – you know –

OTIS

Didn't have a father?

CHET
(*shrugs*)
He's still pissed off about it.

OTIS

When you're his age you'll still be pissed off about him.

Chet nods, looks around.

CHET

So how come you got into all this?

OTIS

These are our people. There were Paynes in Florida, Oklahoma, Piedras Negras – couple of 'em won the whatsit – Congressional Medal of Honor –

CHET

So I'm part-Indian?

OTIS

By blood you are. But blood only means what you let it.

CHET

My father says the day you're born you start from scratch, no breaks and no excuses, and you got to pull yourself up on your own.

OTIS
(*sad*)

Well, he's living proof of that, son. Living proof.

INT. DEL'S OFFICE – DAY

Athena stands at attention as Del sits at his desk, reviewing her record. He lets her stand for a long time before speaking.

DEL

Private Johnson, are you unhappy in the Army?

ATHENA

No, sir.

DEL

Then how would you explain the fact that out of one hundred twenty people we tested, you're the only one who came up positive for drugs?

ATHENA

I'm sorry, sir.

DEL

When you were given the opportunity to enlist, a kind of contract was agreed upon. I think the Army has honored its part of that agreement –

ATHENA

Yes, sir –

DEL

Do you believe in what we're doing here, Private Johnson?

ATHENA

I – I can do the job, sir.

DEL

You don't sound too enthusiastic.

ATHENA

I am, sir.

DEL

What exactly do you think your job is, Private?

ATHENA

Follow orders. Do whatever they say.

DEL

Who's 'they'?

ATHENA

The – the officers.

DEL

And that's the job? Nothing about serving your country –

Athena is confused, hesitates to speak.

These aren't trick questions, Private. You'll be given an
Article 15 and be going into the ADCAP Program one way or
the other. What happens after that is up to you. I'm just
trying to understand how somebody like you thinks.
            (*silence*)
Well?

ATHENA
            (*hesitant*)
You really want to know, sir?

DEL

Please.

ATHENA

It's their country. This is one of the best deals they offer.

Del knows he asked for it, but doesn't like the answer.

DEL

How do you think I got to be a colonel?

ATHENA

Work hard, be good at your job. Sir. Do whatever they tell you.

DEL

Do whatever they tell you –

ATHENA

I mean, follow orders, sir.

DEL

With your attitude, Private, I'm surprised you want to stay in the service.

ATHENA

I do, sir.

DEL

Because it's a job?

ATHENA
(*struggling*)
Outside it's – it's such a mess – it's –

DEL

Chaos.

Athena is sure she's overstepped her rank.

Why do you think they let us in on the 'deal'?

ATHENA

They got people to fight. Arabs, yellow people, whatever. Might as well use us.

DEL

Do you think you've been discriminated against on this post?

ATHENA

No, sir. Not at all.

DEL

Any serious problems with your sergeant or your fellow soldiers?

ATHENA

No, sir. They all been real straight with me.

Del stands, thinking, trying not to bullshit her.

DEL

It works like this, Private – every soldier in a war doesn't have
to believe in what he's fighting for. Most of them fight just to
back up the soldiers in their squad – you try not to get them
killed, try not to get them extra duty, try not to embarrass
yourself in front of them.

He is right in her face now.

Why don't you start with that?

ATHENA

Yes, sir.

DEL

You're dismissed, Private.

ATHENA

Thank you, sir.

*Athena salutes, steps out. Del looks out the window, troubled by the
encounter.*

EXT. BORDER CONTROL – DAY

*A battered car full of Mexican Day Workers rolls toward the Mexican-
side checkpoint.*

INT. CAR – DAY

*Enrique sits squeezed between Workers in the back. The Driver never
stops talking as the Officer waves them through.*

DRIVER
(off-screen)
– *Julia es demasiado flaca para mi – me gusto más mujeres con
algo en frente – o muy altas como Cindy Crofor. Quisiera montar
esa caballa –* [Julia's too skinny for me – I like women with
something up front – or really tall like Cindy Crawford. I'd
like to ride that horse –]

EXT. KINCAID HOUSE – DAY

Sam's car is parked on the street in front of an expensive-looking house in a tree-lined neighborhood.

INT. LIVING ROOM – DAY

Sam's ex-wife, Bunny Kincaid, shuffles across her living room in slippers, crossing to turn off a big-screen TV playing football highlights. Bunny wears shorts, a Houston Oilers sweatshirt and a Dallas Cowboys cap. The living room is like a sports museum – signed footballs, team posters, a bookcase filled with tapes of Texas pro and college football games.

> BUNNY
> The Longhorns gonna kick some serious butt this Saturday, you just watch. We got a kid at tailback from down your way – outta El Indio –

> SAM
> (*off-screen*)
> That's in Maverick County.

She brings us to Sam, sitting uncomfortably beneath a full-sized blowup of Tony Dorsett hurdling a tackler.

BUNNY

Oh. Right. And you're in –?

SAM

Rio.

BUNNY

Right. This kid, Hosea Brown? Does the 40 in 3.4, soft hands, lateral movement – the whole package. Only a sophomore –

SAM

You still going to all the home games?

BUNNY

Well, Daddy's got his box at the stadium, of course, and I'll fly to the Cowboy away games when they're in the Conference. Then there's the high school on Friday nights – West Side got a boy 6'6", 310, moves like a cat. High school, we're talkin'. Guess how much he can bench-press?

SAM

Bunny, you – uhm – you on that same medication?

BUNNY

Do I seem jumpy?

SAM

No, no – you look good. I was just wondering.

BUNNY

Last year was awful rough – Mama passing on and the whole business with OJ – I mean it's not like it was Don Meredith or Roger Staubach or one of our own boys, but it really knocked me for a loop –

SAM

You look good –

BUNNY

– and that squeaker the Aggies dropped to Oklahoma – sonofabitch stepped in some lucky shit before he kicked that goal –

SAM

Yeah, well –

BUNNY

– they hadn't pulled me off that woman I would have jerked a knot in her.

SAM

You were in a fight –

BUNNY

Daddy calls it an 'altercation.' How you doing, Sam? You look skinny.

SAM

Same weight I always was.

BUNNY

You look awful good in that uniform, though.

SAM

Best part of the job.

BUNNY

Daddy hired a pinhead to take your job. He says so himself. Says 'Even my son-in-law was better than this pinhead I got now.'

SAM

Bunny, is that stuff I left in the garage still there?

BUNNY

Least he never called me that. With me, it was always 'high-strung.' 'My Bunny might have done something with her life, she wasn't so high-strung.' Or 'tightly wound,' that was another one. You seeing anyone?

SAM

No. You?

BUNNY

Yeah. Sort of. Daddy rounds 'em up. You aren't talking about money, their beady little eyes go dead.

SAM

You didn't – uhm – you didn't have one of your fires, did
you? The stuff I left in the garage – some of it was my
father's –

BUNNY

You watch the draft this year? 'Course you didn't, idiot
question. They try to make it dramatic, like there's some big
surprise who picks who in the first round? Only they been
working it over with their experts and their computers for
months. Doctor's reports, highlight reels, coaches'
evaluations, psychological profiles – hell, I wouldn't be
surprised if they collected stool samples on these boys, have
'em analysed. All this stuff to pick a football player for your
squad. Compared to that, what you know about the person
you get married to don't amount to diddly, does it?

SAM

Suppose not.

BUNNY

You kind of bought yourself a pig in a poke, didn't you, Sam?
All that time we were first seeing each other you didn't know
I was tightly wound –

SAM

It wasn't just you, Bunny.

BUNNY

No, it wasn't, was it? You didn't exactly throw yourself into it
heart and soul, did you?

he looks at him for an uncomfortably long moment.

Your shit's still in the garage if that's what you came for.

am nods, stands. Bunny is in tears.

350 pounds.

SAM

What?

> BUNNY

This boy from West Side, plays tackle both ways. Bench-presses 350 pounds. You imagine having that much weight on top of you? Pushing down? Be hard to breathe. Hard to swallow.

> SAM

I think they have another fella there to keep it off your chest. A spotter.

> BUNNY

'I only got my little girl now,' he says, 'she's my lifeline.' Then he tells me I can't be in the box anymore if I can't control myself. Sonofabitch don't even watch the damn game, just sits there drinking with his bidness friends, look up at the TV now and then. I do better to sit in the cheap seats with some real football people.

> SAM
> (*edging out*)

You look good, Bunny. It's nice to see you.

> BUNNY
> (*smiles*)

Thanks. I like it when you say that, Sam.

EXT. STREET – CIUDAD LEÓN – DAY

Enrique looks nervously over his shoulder before stepping into a funky apartment building. We tilt up to the second-floor balcony, where a Little Boy is watching the street.

INT. APARTMENT – DAY

There are eight People not including the Little Boy on the balcony. All are securing their possessions – rolling things in blankets, filling shopping bags and grain sacks. Enrique steps in.

> ENRIQUE

Todos estamos? [Everybody here?]

Anselma reaches up from the floor to take his hand.

ANSELMA

Van a disparar a nosotros? [Are they going to shoot at us?]

ENRIQUE

Nadie nos verán. Seramos invisibles. [Nobody's going to see us. We'll be invisible.]

INT. GARAGE – KINCAID HOUSE – DAY

A mess. We start on a campaign poster with Sam's face on it and the legend: 'ONE GOOD DEEDS DESERVES ANOTHER – VOTE SAM DEEDS FOR COUNTY SHERIFF.' We pan to see Sam, who has been digging through piles of old junk, set down the box he was looking for.

Sam pulls out an old holster, a sheaf of real estate and insurance forms, a couple of old paperback Zane Grey Westerns. He pulls out a cracked leather pouch, turns it over – letters fall out. He examines an envelope – no stamp or postmark – pulls a letter out, reads:

SAM

'Dearest Buddy –'

He puts the letter down for a moment, thinks. He needs to know. He picks up the letter again, reads.

INT. OTIS'S HOUSE – EVENING

Carolyn crosses the living room to answer the ring at the front door. Del stands there.

CAROLYN

Hey, it's the General.

DEL

Colonel. Is uhm – is Otis in?

CAROLYN

Come on in –

DEL

If it's too late –

CAROLYN

Come on in.

Del enters the house as if walking into an ambush.

INT. OTIS'S LIVING ROOM – EVENING

Carolyn sits back in the couch, drink in hand, checking Del out.

> CAROLYN
>
> Otis sittin' up with some people at the club. I don't think he'll be long.

CU: Del, uncomfortable, sitting at the edge of an easy chair. He looks at a mounted magazine photo of Otis smiling as he pours hot sauce on a rack of ribs.

> His hot sauce recipe won a contest last year. They sellin' it far away as San Antonio. He got a lot of talent, your father.

Del squirms a bit at the word 'father'.

> DEL
>
> You've been in this house for a while?

> CAROLYN
>
> I been here with him eight years now. He built it when he was with Leora.

> DEL
>
> I never met her.

> CAROLYN
>
> There was a bunch of 'em you never met. Me neither.

Del looks around the living room.

> Let me show you around –

INT. DEN – EVENING

A blowup of a photo of a squad of buffalo soldiers is mounted on the wall.

> CAROLYN
> (off-screen)
> He got into all this cowboys and Indians stuff a while back.

Spend half his time pokin' around in the library way up to Austin.

CU: Del. He looks at something below.

Del's POV – clippings.

We pan slowly over laminated newspaper clippings mounted behind a picture of young Del in a track uniform, holding a vaulting pole. The clippings are about Del making honor rolls, winning a Silver Star in Vietnam, graduating from Officer Candidate School, being named head of this and that in the Army.

> (*off-screen*)
> Kind of like a shrine, isn't it?

Carolyn stands behind, watching Del's face as he looks at the stuff.

DEL

Where'd he get all this?

CAROLYN

Your mother got a brother – Alphonse –

DEL

Uncle Al –

CAROLYN

Otis stood on good terms with the man. Whenever you do something makes the news, he sends it on. When they made you General, Otis just about drove away all our customers going on about it.

DEL

I'm a colonel.

CAROLYN

Yeah, I know. Man made me memorize the whole damn Army chain of command before he'd marry me. So this is a big deal, commander and all?

DEL

It's a small post and they're phasing it out in two years, but I moved up in rank and – well, a command is a command.

CAROLYN

Otis went on like you were that guy who won the Gulf War.
Colin whatsit.

DEL

My mother said he never asked about –

CAROLYN

He never asked *her.*

It's a bit too much for Del.

DEL

Listen, I uh – tell him I came by. Thanks –

We hold on Carolyn as he hurries out. She salutes.

CAROLYN

Catch you later, Colonel.

EXT. RIVER – NIGHT

*People, crouching low, wade across the river toward us. When he gets
close enough to us, we recognize Enrique, nervously leading a group of
Mexican Men, Women and Children to the US side. They are spaced
out in the dark, loosely holding the line Enrique made in one hand and*

holding their bundles high away from the water with the other. Enrique turns as he hears a Woman's cry. The line goes slack, then Nestor steps out of the darkness to join him.

> ENRIQUE

Qué pasó? [What happened?]

> NESTOR

Anselma cayó en las rocas. Creo que la pierna ha sido roto – [Anselma fell on the rocks. I think her leg's broken –]

Two Men struggle forward, supporting Anselma, trying to hold her leg out straight in front of her. She is in a lot of pain.

> *No podemos alcanzar el camión llevando a ella. Hay lugar para esconderla?* [We can't reach the truck if we're carrying her. Is there somewhere to hide her?]

Enrique thinks, trying not to panic, as the others come up around him.

> ENRIQUE

Conozco solamente una persona con casa – [I only know one person with a house –]

> ANSELMA
> (*in pain*)

Está lejos? [Is it far?]

EXT. PATIO – NIGHT

Mercedes sits on her recliner, drink in hand. An old record plays from inside. She is startled by the voice from the dark.

> ENRIQUE
> (*off-screen*)

Señora Cruz?

> MERCEDES
> (*standing*)

Quién es? [Who is it?]

> ENRIQUE

Soy yo, Enrique. No tiene miedo – [It's me, Enrique. Don't be afraid –]

Enrique steps out into the light. His pants are wet and he's scared.

MERCEDES
What are you doing out there? Are you crazy?

ENRIQUE
Ha pasado un accidente muy grave – [There's been a bad accident –]

MERCEDES
In English, Enrique. We're in the United States –

ENRIQUE
I have some friends who have had a accident –

MERCEDES
You have somebody else out there?

ENRIQUE
We was by the river? And I hear my friend callin' for help, and I look and she has falling in the water –

MERCEDES
Don't tell me lies, Enrique. *Qué pasó?*

ENRIQUE
We was crossin' the river –

Nestor appears in the light now, supporting Anselma, who hops awkwardly to move forward.

MERCEDES
Enrique! *Quienes son estos?* How could you bring them here?

ENRIQUE
They need help. Jaime, Anselma – *esta es mi jefa* –

NESTOR
Señora –

MERCEDES
I'll call the Border Patrol, they'll get her to the hospital.

ENRIQUE
No! No puede hacer esto – [You can't do that –]

MERCEDES

You think you're doing these people a favor? What are they going to do? Either they get on welfare or they become criminals –

ENRIQUE

No es la verdad – [That isn't true –]

NESTOR

Con permiso, Señora, la muchacha tiene mucho dolor – [Please, Señora, the girl is in a lot of pain –]

Mercedes grudgingly indicates the lounge chair.

MERCEDES

Siéntase. [Sit.]

NESTOR

Es muy amable. [You're very kind.]

He and Enrique help Anselma into the chair. The girl looks up at Mercedes, frightened.

ANSELMA

Ayúdanos, Señora, por favor. No podemos regresar – [Help us, Señora, please. We can't go back –]

Mercedes looks at Anselma disapprovingly. The girl can't be more than fourteen.

MERCEDES

This girl is a friend of yours?

ENRIQUE

Es mi novia. [She's my girlfriend.]

MERCEDES

I thought you were married!

ENRIQUE

I am marry to the cousin of a friend – but only to be able to live here. This is the mother of my child –

MERCEDES

This girl has a child?

ENRIQUE

We have a daughter.

MERCEDES
(*scornful*)

Típico.

EXT. HOUSE – NIGHT

Sam stands at the front door of a house on the lake, banging on the door.

SAM

Hollis? You in there? Hollis?

EXT. RIVER – NIGHT – 1945

Moonlight kicks off the surface of the water. We hear splashing, the frightened voice of a young woman.

YOUNG MERCEDES
(*off-screen*)
Dónde está? Estoy perdido – [Where are you? I'm lost –]

ELADIO
(*off-screen; distant*)
Aquí! [Here!]

The girl flounders into the shot, wet and scared. Young Mercedes, a teenager not unlike Anselma, is wading thigh-deep in the Rio, lost, scared.

YOUNG MERCEDES
No puedo ver la orilla! [I can't see the bank!]

ELADIO
(*off-screen*)
Aquí! Venga por aquí! [Over here! Come this way!]

Mercedes struggles toward the voice and suddenly a young man becomes visible, standing in the water, holding his hand out for her: Eladio.

YOUNG MERCEDES
Ví a Rosaria arastrado para el corriente – [I saw Rosaria taken away by the current –]

ELADIO

No te molestas. Tenemos a ella. [Don't worry. We've got her.]

He takes her arm, pulls her toward the far shore.

Cómo se llama? [What's your name?]

YOUNG MERCEDES

Mercedes Gonzales Ruiz.

ELADIO
(*smiles*)

Me llamo Eladio Cruz. Bienvenido a Tejas. [Welcome to Texas.]

DISSOLVE TO:

EXT. MERCEDES'S HOUSE – NIGHT

Mercedes is lost in thought as she recalls. She steps into the light by the carport. Enrique and Nestor are propping Anselma's leg up on pillows in the back of Mercedes's old station wagon –

MERCEDES

Rápidamente! Everybody in the world is going to see!

ENRIQUE

Dónde vamos? [Where are we going?]

MERCEDES

A casa de Porfirio Zayas. He used to be a doctor on the other side. Gunshot wounds, fixing babies – if you can pay he can handle it.

ENRIQUE

Señora, anything it costs, I can work –

MERCEDES

Don't worry about it. He owes me some favors.

Enrique turns to Anselma, still frightened in the rear of the station wagon.

ENRIQUE

Séas tranquila, mija.

(*nods to Mercedes*)
Estamos en las manos de Señora Cruz. [Just relax, honey. We're in the hands of Señora Cruz.]

Mercedes starts the car.

MERCEDES
In English, Enrique. In English –

INT. DEL'S HOUSE – DINING ROOM

Del steps in. Chet sits at the table, drawing a cartoon in panels. Del looks over his shoulder for a moment.

Cartoon of tank rolling over barbed wire, cannon and machine-gun blasting away.

DEL
(*off-screen*)
Homework?

Del and Chet.

CHET
I finished that. I'm just messing around.

DEL
Tanks, huh?

CHET
You got to be in the Army, you might as well have something slick to drive.

DEL
So you're going into the Army?

Chet looks at him, not in a good mood, then goes back to his drawing.

CHET
That's the general plan, isn't it?

Del watches for a long moment, thinking.

DEL
(*softly*)
That's up to you.

Chet looks at his father again. This is news to him.

The Army isn't for everybody.

Chet can't quite believe he's hearing this. Del crosses to the refrigerator.

Not that I don't think you'd be good at it, but – you know – I wouldn't be disappointed if you decided to do something else with your life.

CHET

You wouldn't?

DEL

No.

Chet nods, begins to play again, considering the possibilities. Del is making an effort and he doesn't have much practice.

· How's your room shaping up?

CHET

Fine. I'm pretty much moved in.

DEL

Good.

An awkward silence.

CHET
(*tentative*)

Are we going to ever see your father?

DEL

My father.

CHET

Yeah. He lives here, right?

DEL

He does.

Del pulls out some food, watching Chet as he draws.

Maybe we'll clean that thing out back up, have a barbecue next weekend. We could invite him and his wife over.

235

CHET

Cool.

Chet flips the page of his sketchbook.

He makes his own sauce.

EXT. PARKING LOT, BIG O'S – NIGHT

The neon's off, but there are a couple cars in the lot and a light within. Sam pulls into the lot, steps out, approaches the door.

INT. CLUB – NIGHT

The door opens. The place is empty now except for Otis, standing behind the bar, deep in conversation with Hollis, sitting on a stool. Both swivel to look around guiltily as they hear Sam step in.

Reverse: Sam walks in slowly, crossing the floor to bring us back to the two men.

SAM

Fellas.

HOLLIS

Hey, Sam.

SAM

Open late.

OTIS

I'm not open. We were just talking.

SAM

Hollis probably told you we found Charley Wade.

OTIS

Yeah. How about that? People start digging holes in this county, there's no telling what'll come up.

He sits a few stools away from Hollis.

SAM

You two saw it, didn't you? You two saw it when Buddy killed him.

Hollis and Otis look at each other.

I'm gonna find out one way or the other.

HOLLIS

Your father had the finest sense of justice of any man I ever
met –

SAM

Yeah, and my mother was a saint. For fifteen years the whole
damn town knew he had another woman on the side. Stole
ten thousand dollars to set her up in business. But hell, what's
that? You got a problem? Buddy'll fix it. Facing some time in
jail? Buddy'll knock half of it off – if you do what he says,
when he says. You got some business that's not exactly legal?
Talk to Buddy –

HOLLIS

Buddy Deeds –

SAM

Buddy Deeds was a murderer.

He looks at the two older men for a long moment.

That night in the café – he didn't stay long after you left,
did he, Hollis? Maybe he decided he'd gone too far with
Wade, maybe he figured he better not wait for the Sheriff to
get behind him. So he stepped out to see if he could catch
up – and you were here at the club that night, weren't you,
O?

Otis sighs, begins to speak softly.

OTIS

I was here.

*CU: Otis. He turns to look toward the door as he reminisces, and we
pan away with his gaze.*

I'd been running a game on the side after hours – craps, draw
poker on the weekends. Roderick didn't know about it. More
important, Charley Wade didn't know about it, 'cause I
didn't want to cut him in. I suppose I'd been drinking some,

and I was pretty full of myself in those days – but hell, I just didn't expect the man so early –

Sheriff Wade and Young Hollis step in the door and we are back in 1957.

Blues harmonica fades up, wailing from the jukebox. They stop and look at the place.

Their POV – club. Music continues. The club is empty, dark. A light shines from the back room.

INT. BACK ROOM – NIGHT

Music continues. Smoke fills the air and Young Otis sits back laughing, a large pile of money on the table in front of him. The other four black Men at the table aren't doing so well. One by one they all look up past the camera to the door.

CU: Otis. Music continues. Young Otis doesn't see at first, engaged in dealing the cards. Finally, he senses the presence, looks up.

Young Otis's POV: Wade and Hollis. Music continues. Wade stands over the table in the foreground, Young Hollis hanging back in the doorway. Wade is smiling his cold smile, cursing.

CU: Young Otis. Music continues. Otis is trying to look unimpressed.

Extreme CU: Wade's eyes, cold and unblinking. Music continues.

Extreme CU: Wade's mouth, twisted in a snarl as he curses. Music continues.

On Men, table. Music continues. We shoot past Wade's body as the other Men step away from the table, grab their hats, and hurry out the side door. Young Otis is left sitting at the table. Wade starts walking toward him.

CU: Young Otis. Music continues. His eyes following as Wade comes to stand over him.

On Wade and Young Otis. Music continues. Wade grabs the table and violently jerks it over onto Young Otis, cards and money flying.

On Young Hollis. Music continues. Watching squeamishly as Wade goes to work on Young Otis, the overhead light swinging wildly.

INT. BAR-ROOM – NIGHT

Music continues. Young Otis is hurled out of the back room, face bruised and bleeding. Wade follows, then Young Hollis.

Closer. Music continues. Wade puts his gun next to Young Otis's ear, cursing at him. Young Otis gets to his feet, goes behind the bar.

Bar counter. Music continues. Young Otis slaps an envelope full of cash onto the counter.

On Wade. Music continues. He waves his pistol, indicating something behind Otis.

Music continues. We shoot past Wade at the counter as Otis turns and reaches for a cigar box on the shelf behind.

Cigar box. Music continues. Lying open, an old pistol inside of it. Young Otis reaches.

CU: Young Hollis. Music continues. Frowning as he senses something wrong.

On Wade. Music continues. Wade levels his gun at Young Otis's back, then turns to wink at Hollis like he did before he shot Eladio.

On Wade's hand. Music continues. Finger closing around the trigger of the .45.

On Hollis. Music continues. Mouth open in horror.

On Wade. Music continues. Eyes burning as he aims.

On Buddy. Music continues. Stepping in the door, seeing, calls out.

OnYoung Otis. Music continues. Turning to see Buddy.

On Wade. Blam! Thwap! A bullet plows through his neck, knocking him back against the bar. Music continues. His gun falls from his hand.

On Young Otis. Horrified, splattered with the Sheriff's blood. Music continues.

Bar counter. Music continues. Twenty-dollar bills have spilled out of the envelope and are soaking up blood.

CU: Buddy. Calm and hard-eyed. Music continues. As he steps forward, we see his pistol is still in its holster. He reaches out and takes the .45 from Young Hollis's shaking hand, looks him in the eye till Hollis looks back, then looks toward Young Otis.

We pan with his gaze to a CU of Otis, back in the present.

The music fades.

> OTIS
>
> Sheriff Charley had some real big friends in politics then, and if the truth come out it wasn't going to go easy on Hollis.
> *(shrugs)*
> I don't know why I trusted Buddy with it – don't know why he trusted me. The first time I ever talked with him was right there and then with a dead white man leakin' blood on the floor between us. He could charm the scales off a rattler, Buddy Deeds.

Wider: this isn't what Sam was expecting. Hollis watches his face.

> HOLLIS
>
> The three of us cleaned up and took him out by the post and put him under. Can't say I was much help.

> SAM
>
> And the ten thousand?

> HOLLIS
>
> Widow's benefits. He figured it would make the disappearance look better, and that Mexican gal was just scrapin' by after Charley killed her man. They didn't get hooked up till later –

> OTIS
>
> Time went on, people liked the story that we told better than anything the truth might have been.

Sam swivels around on his seat to look at the spot where Charley fell. He's had a lot of information to deal with today.

> HOLLIS
>
> What's the call, Sam?

Sam rolls it over in his mind before answering.

>   SAM
> Don't think the Rangers are likely to find out any more than
> they already have.

>   HOLLIS
> Word gets out who that body was, people are gonna think
> Buddy done it.

Sam gets up.

>   SAM
> Buddy's a goddam legend. He can handle it.

He heads for the door.

> 'Night, fellas.

Hollis and Otis watch him go.

FADE OUT

EXT. DRIVE-IN, WIDE SHOT – MORNING

We see Sam sitting on the hood of his car parked in the deserted drive-in lot, staring up at the ruined screen. Pilar's car rolls in, parks beside him.

Closer: Pilar gets out, kisses Sam, sits by him on the hood.

>   PILAR
> When's the picture start?

Sam looks at her for a moment.

>   SAM
> You gonna tell your mother we been seeing each other?

>   PILAR
> She'll figure it out sooner or later. I don't have to ask
> permission anymore, if that's what you mean.

>   SAM
> You have any idea when your father died? Eladio?

> PILAR
> (*shrugs*)
> Couple months before I was born –

> SAM
> Try a year and a half.

He hands her an old snapshot. Pilar looks at it.

CU: photo. Buddy and Young Mercedes on the lake. Buddy with his shirt off on one end of a sailboat, Mercedes in a bathing suit, both smiling for the camera.

On Sam and Pilar. Pilar hands the photo back to him, tries to be calm.

> PILAR
> I've never seen my mother in a bathing suit before. Didn't know she owned one.

> SAM
> Buddy bought the café for her with money he took from the county.

Pilar looks away, struggling not to cry.

> PILAR
> They can't pull this on me. It isn't fair – I don't believe this –

> SAM
> He paid the hospital bill when you were born. Your mom always calls you 'our beautiful daughter' in the letters she wrote to him.

> PILAR
> From the first time I saw you at school – all those years we were married to other people I always felt like we were connected.

> SAM
> I remember thinking you were the one part of my life Buddy didn't have a piece of –

A silence, both of them wondering what the next move should be.

PILAR

So that's it? You're not going to want to be with me anymore?

Sam knows what he feels but doesn't have the words.

I'm not having any more children. After Amado, I had some complications – I can't get pregnant again, if that's what the rule is about –

SAM

If I met you for the first time today, I'd still want to be with you.

It's what Pilar needed to hear.

PILAR

We start from scratch –

SAM

Yeah –

PILAR

Everything that went before, all that stuff, that history – the hell with it, right?

Pilar takes Sam's hand, kisses him.

Forget the Alamo.

Wide shot of drive-in. Sam and Pilar sit by each other holding hands, looking at the empty screen.

Music, roll credits.